BERLITZ®

ISTRIA
and Croatian Coast

1987/1988 Edition

By the staff of Berlitz Guides
A Macmillan Company

Berlitz Trademark Reg. U.S. Patent Office and other countries.
Marca Registrada. Library of Congress Catalog Card No. 76-21 366.

Printed in Switzerland by Weber S.A., Bienne.

8th Printing
1987/1988 Edition

How to use our guide

- All the practical information, hints and tips that you will need before and during the trip start on page 95.

- For general background, see the sections The Region and the People, p. 6, and A Brief History, p. 11.

- All the sights to see are listed between pages 18 and 71.

  ![Berlitz symbol] Our own choice of sights most highly recommended are pinpointed by the Berlitz traveller symbol.

- Entertainment, nightlife and all other leisure activities are described between pages 72 and 84, while information on restaurants and cuisine is to be found on pages 84 to 94.

- Finally, there is an index at the back of the book, pp. 126–128.

Although we make every effort to ensure the accuracy of all the information in this book, changes occur incessantly. We cannot therefore take responsibility for facts, prices, addresses and circumstances in general that are constantly subject to alteration. Our guides are updated on a regular basis as we reprint, and we are always grateful to readers who let us know of any errors, changes or serious omissions they come across.

Text: Madge Tomašević
Photography: Erling Mandelmann
Layout: Doris Haldemann
We would like to thank Naum R. Dimitrijević, Valerie Majkus and the Yugoslav National Tourist Office for their assistance in the preparation of this book.
Cartography: Falk-Verlag, Hamburg

Contents

Cover picture: Roman arena, Pula

This is Istria

The Region and the People

Heart-shaped Istria, "gateway to the Adriatic", attracts more foreign visitors than any other region of Yugoslavia. Geography helps.

Italians flock across the border on weekends for cheap, wholesome food and uncrowded, unpolluted bathing. A day's drive brings Austrians and many Germans to pine-clad sunny shores and quaint old towns. And now jet-loads of travellers sweep in from northern Europe and North America. Unhurried tourists can investigate the world of contrasts beyond the beaches.

In the north, the stark limestone countryside is dotted with stunted trees, mysterious vanishing rivers and caves bedecked with stalactites and stalagmites. On the eastern coast, Mount Učka rises above the narrow, verdant seaboard, alive with resorts. The densely wooded valleys of the central area give way to bare uplands, rich vineyards or rust-red farmland. Here every hill bears traces of history—a tiny

ITALIA

Ljubljana

Trieste

Koper

Piran

ISTRA

Mirna   Fojba

Novigrad   Motovun

Poreč

Rovinj

Opatija   Rijeka

Krk

K.VARNER

Cres

Pula

JADRANSKO   MORE

9th-century church, a prehistoric burial mound, a half-deserted village or ruined castle. On the western shore of Istria, tens of thousands of tourists can bask and bathe in countless coves and bays without that crowded feeling.

Yugoslavia enjoys more than 1,200 miles of coastline (not counting the proverbial thousand islands, rocks and reefs). But it is Istria that boasts the most agreeable climate. While the summer sun may scorch more southerly resorts, Opatija basks in perfection (average daily high and low temperatures in July: 82°F and 66°F). At the same time, the summer sea tends to be warmer here—refreshing, not challenging.

Tourism has made little impact on the interior of the peninsula. In fact, only 6 per cent of the labour force works in tourism and trade. Farming remains the principal source of livelihood, as it has since the Bronze Age when an Illyrian tribe called the Histri settled here. They also gave the region its name. Other Illyrians—the Liburnians of Istria's east coast —were skilled seamen and shipbuilders; the Romans adopted the design of their swift galleys. The shipbuilding tradition continues today in the great yards of Pula and Rijeka.

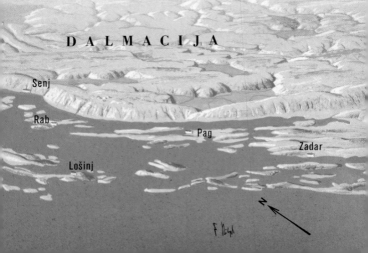

DALMACIJA

Senj

Rab

Pag

Zadar

Lošinj

N

F. Nigl

South of Rijeka, the rugged grey wall of the Velebit range soars up from the sea, leaving scant room for settlements at its base. Here the Adriatic Highway snakes toward Crikvenica, a smaller Opatija with the same kind of *fin de siècle* charm. Farther south the forbidding fortifications of Senj recall the turbulent past when pirates terrorized Adriatic shipping, Venetian and Turkish alike. Though seafaring and fishing continue to provide jobs along the coast and on the islands, tourists have brought new prosperity to many fishing villages on this sun-baked rocky shore.

The sparkling Kvarner Gulf separates Istria from the Croatian Littoral. The gulf's four main islands—Cres, Lošinj, Krk and Rab—have fine sandy beaches along with exciting underwater fishing. A boat trip from any of the big four to one of the sparsely populated smaller islands, such as Unije, Susak or Silba, takes you as far from civilization as most tourists care to venture.

By contrast, big resorts like Opatija, Poreč and Crikvenica offer entertainment and nightlife for all tastes. You're never more than 50 kilometres from a casino here. In elegant restaurants or humble cafés, you'll enjoy Mediterranean, Austrian or Serbian cuisine served with cheap but good local wines.

Don't neglect two very important aspects of Istria during your visit: the splendours of history and art and the people themselves. Take in highlights like the Roman amphitheatre of Pula, the 6th-century basilica of Poreč with its glittering mosaics, fresco-covered village churches all over Istria and the graceful campaniles of Rab. And seek out the gregarious Yugoslavs, people with a highly developed sense of national pride, eager to show off local attractions. If you're interested, ask them to explain the workings of their unique form of socialism based on worker management and local self-government. Most visitors, however, see few external signs of a different social system.

Our guide deals with two of Yugoslavia's six republics—Slovenia and Croatia. If the languages confound you, try Italian, German or English. The people will meet you more than half way across the language barrier. It's all part of the traditional hospitality. You'll be treated with friendly courtesy, but not servility, whether you stay at a luxury hotel or a simple guest house. The Slovenes and Croats,

8

On many inland Istrian farms, age-old agricultural techniques linger.

both South Slavs, differ in language (Slovenian and Serbo-Croatian) and to some extent in temperament. Through some eight centuries of Hapsburg rule, the million or so Slovenes clung tenaciously to their national identity. Considered the most industrious and efficient of the Yugoslavs, they enjoy the highest living standard in the country. The Croats, numbering over 4 million, are spread out from the Pannonian Plain to the Adriatic. The northern Croats of Zagreb are

9

quite polished and formal in manner. While along the coast, you'll find the talkative Dalmatians, fond of wine, women and song, a Mediterranean breed.

Yugoslavia claims Europe's loveliest coastline. It was almost undiscovered until about 20 years ago, when the more adventurous tourists struck out eastward to escape crowds and commercialization. Though the good news has inevitably spread, overcrowding is still a very distant threat.

Local taste favours mackerel and sardines; below: *native ingenuity finds solutions to many problems.*

A Brief History

The history of Yugoslavia begins thousands of years ago. Yet its peoples have formed one state only since 1918. And its very name, Yugoslavia, dates back less than 50 years.

The Adriatic shores were already inhabited in the Stone Age, perhaps 5,000 years ago. Illyrian tribes settled here during the Bronze and Iron Ages.

In the 4th century B.C., the Greeks set up trading posts on the mainland and nearby islands. By the 1st century A.D., Roman armies had conquered both the Greeks and the Illyrians. Roman rule united the territory now known as Yugoslavia—a feat that was not to be accomplished again for 1,500 years.

The split in the Roman empire towards the end of the 4th century A.D. affected all of the ancient world. It had a major impact on the Balkans. Present-day Serbia, Macedonia, Montenegro and most of Bosnia-Herzegovina were absorbed by the eastern empire of Constantinople; Slovenia, Croatia and Dalmatia went under the wing of Rome. The cultural and religious gulf widened during the Middle Ages when the western, Catholic regions fell, in turn, under Hungarian, Venetian and Austrian rule, while the Orthodox areas were swallowed up by the Turkish empire. Despite the political unification of modern Yugoslavia, these ancient divisions have not entirely been erased.

The Dark Ages

The Dark Ages were harsh in Yugoslavia. Hordes of invaders—infamous tribes like the Goths, Huns and Vandals—swept over the land. No less barbarous were the Avars, founders of the first Mogul empire. Probably the first Slavs to set foot in Yugoslavia were warriors attached to the Avar armies.

From plunder, the invaders gradually turned to more peaceful occupations. The romanized Illyrians and the descendants of Roman settlers living along the coast either fled to the islands or crowded for safety into fortified towns. The Slavs, Croats and Slovenes, were left to farm the countryside—the origin of an ethnic division that still persists to a certain degree in Istria.

Less protected on the landside than the rest of the coast, Istria was repeatedly devastated by foreign invasion and internal strife. After periods of Byzantine, Lombard and **11**

Frankish rule, an uneasy division of power was effected. Venice exercised a loose control over the cities on the west coast and German feudal lords (and later the Austrian Hapsburgs) ruled the interior and the east coast.

Catastrophe was an everyday event. Venice's wars, Turkish invasion, revolts, pirate raids and various epidemics decimated the population. Pula, which boasted 30,000 inhabitants in Roman times, was reduced to 300 by the mid-17th century. To reinforce their defences against the Turks, Slavs from other parts of the Balkans were encouraged to settle in the deserted Istrian countryside.

In Dalmatia, however, the energetic Croats gradually built up a strong, thriving state supported by a powerful navy. In 924, Pope John X crowned Tomislav the first king of Croatia. The kingdom lasted for almost 200 years, until its union with Hungary.

Venetian Dominance
In the 15th century, through a combination of sea power, diplomacy and financial dealing, Venice gained control over most of the coast. This brought a period of relative tranquillity to the cities, and art and architecture flourished. But the great days of Venice were already passing as the discovery of the New World reduced the importance of Mediterranean trade routes. Venice's hold in the Adriatic weakened, and Croatia, caught between Austria and the Turks, had some rough years.

In the year 1797, the Venetian republic changed hands twice: first Napoleon and then Austria held sway. Dalmatia also became part of the Hapsburg empire, remaining in Austrian hands until World War I—except for one brief and dramatic interlude in 1809 when Napoleon took over. Following the example of the Caesars, Bonaparte renamed Dalmatia the Illyrian Province, but he showed less respect for tradition in abolishing the historical independence of the city republics.

When Napoleon met his Waterloo in 1815, Austria reasserted control. Under the new regime, the prosperous Italian minority enjoyed a favoured position, which the Croats and Slovenes naturally resented. Bad feeling between Italians and Yugoslavs continued into the 20th century, involving a series of border disputes that have only recently been settled.

Croatian feeling against the

Magyars, who controlled the Croats, Slovenes and Serbs in the Hapsburg empire, reached acute proportions in the latter part of the 19th century. The Hungarians attempted to force magyarization, enraging the people and inciting the spread of pan-Slavism. The independent state of Serbia served as an inspiration for ideas of

Winged lion of St. Mark remains from days of Venetian rule; below: the 6th-century basilica of Poreč.

South Slav autonomy, even independence.

In time, the explosive situation, which grew worse as the Hapsburg regime became feeble and more desperate, affected all of European history. On June 28, 1914, Archduke Franz Ferdinand, heir to the Hapsburg empire, was assassinated in the Bosnian city of Sarajevo. The Serbian government was accused of connivance in the plot. After issuing a humiliating ultimatum which Serbia couldn't accept, and urged on by a Germany which believed in dealing from strength, Austria-Hungary declared war, hoping to expand its Balkan territories. The other big powers were drawn in, and Europe marched into the horrors of World War I.

After heroically checking the Austro-Hungarian advance for over a year and, incidentally, winning the first allied victory of the war at Cer, the exhausted Serbian armies, weakened by a typhoid epidemic, short of supplies and attacked from the rear by Bulgaria, were forced to retreat across the Albanian mountains to Corfu. It was here that the concept of a united Yugoslavia, the long-cherished dream of South Slavs, formally took shape. In mid-summer 1917, representatives of Serbia, Croatia, Slovenia and Montenegro signed the Corfu Declaration calling for the formation of a single state under the Serbian crown in which all Yugoslav peoples would enjoy complete equality.

Tumultuous Search for Unity
The years between the world wars made Yugoslavia the kind of country which inspired clichés about the Balkan tinderbox. Italian troops, implementing a secret treaty of 1915 in which Britain, France and Rus-

Slow but sure means of transport.

sia promised these regions to Italy as part of its reward for joining the allies in the war, occupied Istria and parts of the Dalmatian coast. In addition, failure by the Serbian-dominated government to meet the terms of the Corfu Declaration regarding national equality was a source of bitterness and discord within the young state. In 1928, the Croatian opposition leader was shot down in parliament; the following year King Alexander proclaimed a royal dictatorship, banning all political parties and nationalist organizations. It was at this time that the country's name was changed to Yugoslavia. The world depression of the early 1930s was particularly hard on Yugoslavia's economy; the unemployment rate boiled to an explosive 40 per cent. In 1934, on a state visit to France, King Alexander was assassinated by a man working for Macedonian and Croatian separatist groups.

Staggered by these disasters, and surrounded by the growing menace of Hitler and Mussolini, Yugoslavia tried to steer clear of Europe's approaching confrontations. But protestations of neutrality couldn't match the pressures. In March 1941, Prince Paul, the regent, went to Hitler's Berchtesgaden

Yugoslav Mosaic

The Socialist Federal Republic of Yugoslavia is a federation of six republics, each with its own government, largely corresponding to the regions inhabited by the various South Slav nations. Its population of 21 million lives in an area roughly the size of Great Britain, but speaks three different languages and writes in two different alphabets.

The biggest city and federal capital, Belgrade (Beograd), is also capital of Serbia, the largest republic, a region rich in farmland and natural resources. The second largest republic, Croatia (Hrvatska), stretches from the northern plain to the sea. It boasts a good part of Yugoslavia's industry. In descending order of size, next comes mountainous Bosnia-Herzegovina, then Macedonia and Slovenia (where they speak, naturally, Macedonian and Slovenian) and Montenegro (Crna Gora). In this highly decentralized system, the basic government unit is the local commune (općina).

15

hideaway for a secret audience with the *Führer*. The resulting agreements pledged Yugoslavia's support for the Axis in return for the promise of Salonika (Greek Macedonia). Irate Yugoslavs sent Paul packing into exile within a matter of days. Under popular pressure, the new government renounced the Axis pact, so enraging Hitler that he declared he would wipe Yugoslavia off the map.

On April 6, 1941, without a formal declaration of war, the *Luftwaffe* bombed Belgrade; Axis troops rolled across five frontiers. Ill-prepared and betrayed, the defending armies of young King Peter capitulated within ten days. As Peter and his top men fled to exile, Yugoslavia's foes swooped on the luckless country. Germany, Italy, Bulgaria, Hungary and Albania dismembered most of the territory; the remainder fell under the rule of collaborators.

But the vanquished struck back. Guerilla bands soon organized large-scale resistance activities. Initially, in 1941 the communist-led Partisans and royalist Chetniks under Col. Draža Mihajlović agreed to join forces against the enemy. But it soon became apparent that they were too incompatible politically to cooperate. Evidence increased that

Chetniks were assisting the Germans. When the Allies began dropping supplies in 1943, it was only to the Partisans' National Liberation Army, commanded by Josip Broz Tito. The triumphant uphill fight of the Partisans in pinning down tens of thousands of enemy troops and finally liberating their own country has been widely told. The price the Yugoslavs paid for their liberty was high—the loss of over 1,700,000 lives.

A Republic Proclaimed

At the end of 1943, Tito was named marshal of Yugoslavia and president of the National Liberation Committee (a provisional government). As peacetime leader of a new Yugoslavia—proclaimed a socialist federal republic on November 29, 1945—he totally altered the course of his country's economic and political life. In 1948 Yugoslavia broke with Stalin, abandoning Soviet tutelage to create a distinctive brand of socialism based on worker management and self-governing communes. The vexing nationalities question was met by giving each of the six republics almost complete autonomy in its internal affairs. The foreign policy of non-alignment (of which President Tito

Rijeka's port and shipyards are important to region's prosperity.

was a founder) catapulted Yugoslavia to an international significance far beyond its size or wealth. With the death of Tito in 1980 Yugoslavia turned to the task of consolidating the real-life achievements of the legendary national leader.

Who's the Boss?

If you're unfamiliar with the Yugoslav system, you may wonder who actually owns the hotel you're staying in and the shops and cafés you patronize. A Yugoslav will usually tell you they're "socially owned" and will be offended if you confuse this with the centralized state ownership system of the Soviet Union.

In Yugoslavia, hotels and factories, and most shops, belong to the whole community. They are managed by the people who work in them through their workers' councils and the executives they appoint. This "worker management" system was designed to promote efficiency and stimulate competition. It has its pros and cons, but by and large it works better than sceptics forecast when it was introduced in the country in the late 1940s.

Private enterprise is confined to very small businesses. You'll come across plenty of private cafés, hairdressers, cake shops and repair shops of all kinds. You'll be able to recognize them by the abbrevation *vl.* and the owner's name on the shop (*vl.* = *vlasnik* = proprietor).

Where to Go

Istria's West Coast

Half modern, bustling port and industrial centre, half medieval city, **Koper,** the largest town of Slovenian Istria, successfully leads a double life. Motoring into Istria from Trieste (20 km. away) or Ljubljana (118 km.), those in a hurry may be inclined to bypass the city, deterred by the puce-coloured, high-rise apartment buildings visible across the causeway linking Koper with the road south. However, the delightful main square of the old town is one of the architectural gems of Istria.

Founded by the Greeks on an island that was later made into a peninsula, Koper passed through Roman and Slav hands before being taken over by the Venetians in the 13th century. The carved lion of St. Mark is much in evidence. By the 16th century, Koper had become the chief town of the region. Then a plague epidemic in 1551 wiped out two-thirds of its population, and the city never regained its former prosperity. After centuries of stagnation, it began to revive in 1954 when it became part of Yugoslavia under the London Agreement.

From the steamer quay, follow Kidričeva Street (most of it 16th century), which is usually crowded with shoppers and tourists. The imposing Baroque **Belgramoni-Tacco Palace,** housing the Regional Art and Historical Museum, has some paintings by, among others, Gentile Bellini and Vittore Carpaccio. The latter was reputedly a resident, if not a native, of the town. All streets in Koper lead to the **main square** *(Titov trg).* There, in the shady arcade of the elegant pillared **Loggia** *(Loža),* built in Venetian Gothic style, you can sip the local Refoško red wine while admiring the **Praetorian Palace** *(Pretorova palača)* across the square. Once the residence of the Venetian governor, now the law courts, it started out in the 13th century as two buildings. They were joined 200 years later, but that wasn't the end of it. Local builders went on to add coats-of-arms, governors' busts, decorative battlements, statues and inscriptions until they'd created an architectural extravagance fit for an Italian opera set.

The **cathedral** *(Stolnica)* is Gothic at the bottom and Renaissance above. It took a century to build and was dedicated to an obscure St. Nazarius. Its

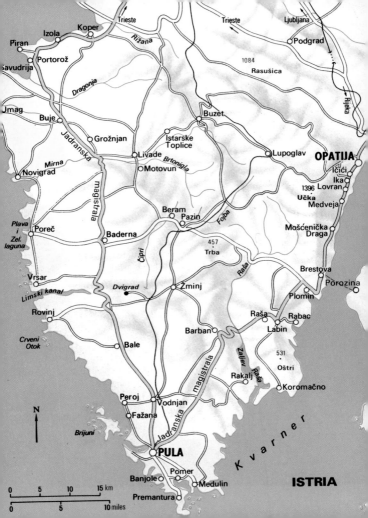

Baroque interior contains the saint's sarcophagus and some paintings by Carpaccio. From the top of the massive 13th-century campanile, which once served as a watch tower, you have an intriguing view of Koper's old streets radiating from the square. The most interesting is narrow Čevljarska, the main shopping street, entered through an archway in the Praetorian Palace.

Koper's many butchers' shops cater in part to Italians who cross the border to save on the weekly food bill. However, they often squander this economy by staying on for the weekend. The Yugoslavs, in turn, slip over to Trieste for their fashionable gear. Traffic at the nearest frontier post, Škofije, is heavy but usually flows smoothly. Its railway and bus station, though out-

Koper's Venetian governor used to reside in this extravagant palace.

side the town centre, is modern and efficient.

In addition to tourism and trade, Koper prospers from its port (Slovenia's main sea outlet) and industry (car assembly and motorscooter manufacture).

Though you can bathe at Koper itself, most people prefer to go across the bay to ŽUSTERNA or better still to ANKARAN (20 minutes by motorboat), with its half-mile, sandy-bottomed beach and excellent camping site.

Going south from Koper, the main road hugs the coastline to IZOLA, 7 kilometres away. As its name suggests, Izola was built on an island, later linked to the mainland. A busy fishing port with considerable industry (canning, toys), it has managed to preserve its old quarter unspoilt. The most striking building is the rococo **Besenghi Palace,** a wedding-cake confection of stucco and wrought iron. Not far away is the 16th-century parish church of Sveti Mavro, which houses some notable old masters (Girolamo da Santacroce, Palma Giovane). There's bathing around the town and at nearby Simonov Bay.

For elegant hotels in a setting of sub-tropical flowers, sophisticated entertainment and a long sandy beach, choose **Portorož,** the "port of roses" (14 km. from Koper). Belted by terraced hills covered with vines, olive trees and cypresses, this sheltered bay enjoys a mild climate year-round, which attracted tourists early in the century. The splendidly ornate edifice where Franz Lehar reputedly wrote *The Merry Widow* has been joined by modern hotels offering every luxury. There's also a casino —for non-Yugoslavs only.

On nearby Seća point, outstanding modern sculptures are permanently on view in a lovely park. Artists from many

Finding Your Way	
centar grada	city centre
crkva	church
kaštel	castle
kolodvor	railway station
muzej	museum
pjaca, placa	square
plaža	beach
obala	quay
staza	footpath
trg	square
tržnica	market
tvrdjava	fort
ulica	street
vrata	gate
desno	right
levo	left
pravo	straight ahead

lands have donated them after participating in the *Forma Viva* sculpture exhibition held here each summer.

Piran, just 3 kilometres north of Portorož but five centuries away in atmosphere, is one of the most beautiful Venetian towns on the Yugoslav coast.

Piran was founded by refugees from Aquileia, the Roman city across the Adriatic that was devastated by barbarians in the 6th century. A buccaneers' strong-hold in the early Middle Ages, its fortifications were gradually extended inland as the settlement spread. Like other Istrian coastal towns, it was under Venetian rule from the 13th century until 1797, though it enjoyed a certain degree of autonomy.

Facing the harbour, the present town centre, **Tartinijev trg,** is named after the violinist and composer Giuseppe Tartini, who was born here. The handsome red building with lacey stone-carving, dating from the 15th century, bears the defiant motto: *Lassa pur dir* (Let them talk!). The story goes that a rich Venetian built the house for his mistress. It now serves, less romantically, as the tourist office. The street behind leads to Piran's largest church, **St. George's** *(Sveti Juraj),* perched on a bluff with a breathtaking view. In an effort to keep up with Venice, the people of Piran modelled its campanile on the one in Piazza San Marco.

From Tartini Square, walk west along the seafront, past bathers, lively cafés and pastel-washed houses to the Moorish-style lighthouse. Return through the narrow winding streets of the Old Quarter. Prvomajski trg, the former town centre, has a great Baroque cistern, Piran's source of fresh water in times past. Besides interesting old buildings, Piran's attractions include a theatre, an aquarium and an art gallery. The Town and Maritime Museum has some good paintings, a Tartini room and several outstanding 18th-century model sailing ships.

You can bathe off the rocks and promenade surrounding the town and at Fijesa cove, 1 kilometre to the north.

Leaving Piran and Portorož, the road skirts the broad salt pans of SEČOVLJE, then crosses the River Dragonja into Croatia. This is "red Istria" (red not from its political leanings,

Piran: an Istrian echo of Venice, complete with copied campanile.

but from the vivid colour of its soil), a region famous for the white Malvazija and red Teran wines. At this point, you can turn right on the coast road to Savudrija and Umag, or follow the faster inland route (A 2) to Buje. The two roads, both paved, eventually meet up near Rovinj.

Set on a flat limestone shore with pine woods, good hotels and excellent camping sites, the fishing village of SAVUDRIJA (25 km. from Portorož) is a delightful spot. Its lighthouse, the westernmost point of the Balkans, is one of the tallest in the Adriatic. Nearby lie the remains of the Roman settlement of Šipar. Probably destroyed by pirates in the 9th century, it's now half submerged, startling proof that the eastern Adriatic coast is sinking about an inch every hundred years.

A pretty medieval village standing on a promontory, UMAG (8 km. south of Savudrija) has developed recently into a lively resort. It offers half a dozen good hotels (one with a casino), attractive bungalows and villas, tourist villages and just about everything in the way of sports, entertainment and shopping. These facilities are concentrated around PUNTA (2 km. to the north) and KATORO (4 km. to the north). The most imposing building in Umag itself is the 18th-century Baroque church on the main square.

Inland, 13 kilometres east of Umag, lies BUJE, a charming hilltop town with medieval streets and well-preserved battlements. Buje is noted for its September wine festival. A flourishing international gathering of young musicians *(Jeunesses musicales)* is held in nearby GROŽNJAN. In the summer, the strains of string quartets and choirs echo through its narrow streets.

Further inland is the spa of ISTARSKE TOPLICE (also known as Sveti Stjepan), where the Romans went to care for their rheumatism in the sulphurous hot springs.

Novigrad (16 km. south of Umag) means new town. It's been "new" since the Byzantines took over the Roman town and called it Neapolis. When the Croats settled here in the 6th century, they merely translated the name, as did the Venetians when they moved in. Novigrad was once an important port that flourished on timber brought from inland Istria down the River Mirna. Only fragments of the town ramparts survive from the sacking by the Turks in 1687.

Now a peaceful place with old-world charm, it contains some fine buildings. The Baroque basilican church *(Sveti Pelagije)* holds the relics of St. Pelagius (a 3rd-century child martyr) in the crypt below the altar. In the attractive Urizzi Mansion, antique and medieval sculpture and stone carvings are displayed. Novigrad has good town beaches. A kilometre away there's a

Two Poreč window views–a quiet interior and an imposing panorama.

hotel and camping complex in a pine wood.

South of Novigrad, the road crosses the marshy estuary of the Mirna. Beyond, a right-hand turning leads to the LANTERNA peninsula, an area of luxuriant aromatic shrubs and pines surrounded by incredibly clear sea. Its natural beauty has been exploited with taste and care. Discreetly enclosed in one cove is the Solaris naturist village.

Thrusting out into the sea on its narrow peninsula, the charming old town of **Poreč** (16 km. from Novigrad) has bypassed both Opatija and Dubrovnik as Yugoslavia's most popular resort.

Hotels, holiday villages, bungalows and camps are neatly tucked away in pine-fringed bays and wooded promontories. Only from the sea is the extent of Poreč's tourist boom apparent. Thanks to the quirks of the coastline, there's still plenty of space for solitary walks and bathing.

A stroll through Poreč is like a quick course in European architecture. From the modern main square *(Trg slobode)*

Glittering mosaics adorn the Poreč basilica; below: *in town museum.*

overlooked by a Baroque church dedicated to St. Mary *(Gospa od andjela)*, you pass a 13th-century, five-sided tower, a remnant of the former city walls. The smooth flagstones of shady Dekumanova Street run straight as an arrow between Romanesque and Gothic mansions with elaborately carved windows. This was one of the two main streets of the town that grew out of a Roman camp of the 2nd century B.C.

The first narrow side street on your left leads to the covered market—the place for fresh fruit, vegetables and fish. The next turning on your right leads to Poreč's greatest glory: the **basilica** of Bishop Euphrasius *(Eufrazijeva bazilika)*, built by a powerful Byzantine prelate in the 6th century on top of previous churches. The basilica, complete with its atrium and baptistery, ranks among the most perfectly preserved of Early Christian churches. Its glittering gold mosaics rival those of Ravenna or Istanbul. Notice the Virgin and Child above the altar and Bishop Euphrasius holding a somewhat lopsided model of the church. If you detect an unholy glint in his eye, you may be right: the pope accused him of incest, adultery and murder, not to mention heresy.

His monogram inscribed on the pillars (originally Roman) and above the main door indicates a certain lack of Christian humility. Among the church's other treasures is the magnificent ciborium (canopy) with Venetian mosaics.

Climb the adjoining campanile for a bird's-eye view of the whole basilica, including the bishop's palace, the orange-tiled roofs of Poreč and the glorious coastline.

Strolling further along Dekumanova Street, past ice-cream parlours, souvenir boutiques and well-stocked food shops in the ground floors of medieval townhouses, you come to **Marafor Square** (Forum of Mars), with the scanty remains of two Roman temples. The one on the left, thought to be dedicated to Mars, is the largest Roman temple in Istria. The altar of the other, the temple of Neptune, now sits in the Town Museum *(Gradski muzej)*, housed in an 18th-century Baroque palace on Dekumanova Street.

Cardo Maximus Street leads down to the main sea-front promenade *(Obala Maršala Tita)*, edged by hotels, seafood restaurants and cafés. The colourful harbour, crowded with luxury yachts and fishing **27** boats, is sheltered from winds by the green island of SVETI NIKOLA (St. Nicholas), a five-minute boat ride away. There you can stay in an 18th-century mansion surrounded by sub-tropical gardens or enjoy the privacy of your own bungalow.

Seven kilometres south of Poreč lie the BLUE LAGOON *(Plava laguna)* and GREEN LAGOON *(Zelena laguna),* developments with accommodation for every taste and pocket. And the area has an unsurpassed variety of sports facilities—sailing, speed-boating, skin-diving, horse-riding, tennis, bowling, cycling, even kite-skiing. If you don't have your own equipment, you can hire it on the spot. The bigger hotels have their own pools (some with heated sea-water for off-season visitors). But there's also the possibility of lazing around in the sun, sampling the local wine.

In the evening, you can dine to a chorus of tree crickets, dance under the stars or attend a concert. Bach in the basilica is unforgettable. Or you may prefer folk songs and dances in the summer theatre *(Ljetna Pozornica).* Regular bus services link the lagoons with Poreč and with the PICAL tourist village and MATERADA beach complex north of Poreč.

The real Istria is not glittering hotels, camping sites and yacht marinas. A few miles inland from Poreč, the rural way of life—wine, fruit and maize crops, ploughs drawn by wide-horned white oxen—seems scarcely to have changed for centuries. Many towns and villages have a deserted air nowadays as the young people gravitate to jobs along the coast.

The most attractive of the ancient hilltop towns scattered over central Istria is **Motovun,** a 27-kilometre excursion from Poreč. A dinner of local specialities, served in front of the castle that is now a hotel, comes with the coach trip. The road corkscrews around a 900-foot hill up to the towering walls and gate. The 13th-century inner gateway through the oldest town hall of Istria leads to a flagstone square. Around it are the *kaštel,* an imposing Renaissance church and a 15th-century belfry.

Take a walk around the encircling battlements for views of the Mirna river in the valley below, running between oak forests famed for their truffles. In the distance, the Ćićarija and Učka mountains rise 4,600 feet high.

An asphalt road leads south to Pazin passing BERAM,

known for its Gothic **frescoes** —*Dance of Death* and *Adoration of the Magi*—in the little church of St. Mary *(Sveta Marija na Škriljinah)*.

A frontier town for centuries, PAZIN (32 km. from Poreč) has more of an Austrian than a Venetian feeling. The Germanic counts of Pazin built their castle on the edge of cliffs that plunge straight down to a **chasm** where a whole river vanishes underground. The setting inspired Jules Verne to pitch one of his characters, Mathias Sandorf, over the battlements. He disappeared into the underground river and later reappeared on the coast— technically impossible, but a great flight of fanciful fiction.

Now the castle serves as an Ethnographical and Historical Museum.

Sailing, skin-diving and water-skiing are top sports at Plava Laguna.

Pazin castle once marked limits of Venetian and Austrian territory.

VRSAR (9 km. south of Poreč) is more than a village, less than a town. Founded by the Romans, it once was the summer residence of the mighty bishops of Poreč. The walled nucleus of Vrsar tops a hill above a protected cove. From the harbour, climb past the cottages of fishermen, wine-growers and artists and through the town gates to the dilapidated little piazza and the abandoned bishop's castle.

The winding shore of sand and pebble explains Vrsar's growing success as a bathing resort, mostly given over to naturists. The off-shore island of KUVERSADA has also become a very large centre for naturists. Another lies a bit further south, at the mouth of the **Limski kanal,** a spectacu-lar 6-mile inlet set between sheer cliffs. This Adriatic "fjord" has been used by film-makers for Nordic location shots.

The old houses of **Rovinj** (27 km. from Vrsar) cluster on rocks and clamber up the slopes of an islet that was linked to the mainland only 200 years ago. The monumental Baroque **Church of St. Euphemia** crowns the summit. Built on the site of two earlier churches, Sveta Eufemija has fragments of a 14th-century marble relief of the patron saint. From its 197-foot bell tower, look down on the winding streets, the wide harbour edged by the colourful awnings of the cafés and in the distance 13 little islands clustered by the shore.

The Undercover Story
Naturists—more often called nudists by the un-initiated—rate red-carpet treatment in Yugoslavia. Official policy considers them a wholesome element. The largest naturist centre in Europe is located on the Istrian coast at Kuversada, near Vrsar—a naked city of over one square mile. Every August, aspiring beauty queens compete for the title of Miss Kuversada, and, for

once, the judges display as much of their physique as the contestants.

You'll find other naturist beaches in Istria near Umag (Katoro), Poreč (at Lanterna, Červar and Funtana), Rovinj (Valalta, Rubin, Monsena and Crveni otok) and Medulin (two camps). The Kvarner Islands also have attractive naturist reserves.

An FKK sign indicates a beach or camp intended for these sun-worshippers who, for the most part, prefer to spend their holidays under canvas.

A light-hearted town with a large Italian minority, Rovinj is a Yugoslav St. Tropez. Many artists, writers and actors have summer homes here.

Rovinj has had a much more troubled history than its present carefree atmosphere would suggest. Despite strong defences, it was sacked in turn by Dalmatian, Genoese and Uskok pirates. It was periodically ravaged by the plague as well. After enjoying relative prosperity as a port under Venetian rule, it was eclipsed by Pula and Trieste. The Austrians gave Rovinj a boost in the 19th century by opening a large tobacco factory and the Marine Biology Institute here. Both still operate.

In the main square *(Trg Maršala Tita)* off the harbour, the ornate Balbi Arch (1680) was one of the three town gates. The Baroque town hall now houses the Gradski Muzej with old and modern paintings, a library and period furniture. Pass under the Balbi Arch and wander through the old Venetian quarter with its quaint piazzas and steep lanes. After St. Benedict's Gate *(Vrata Svetog Benedikta)*, the street runs parallel to the sea around to the rocks and tiny pebble coves where you can swim.

The square on the north side of town *(Trg Valdibora)* is a clutter of stalls laden with fruit, vegetables, carved and woven souvenirs. The Gandusio Theatre on one side faces a striking war memorial by the sea.

Botanists and nature lovers will want to visit the large park with rare Mediterranean flora on the Muntrav promontory, south of Rovinj. The old quarries nearby once supplied stone for the Doge's Palace in Venice.

Most of Rovinj's hotels (one with a casino) are situated along the pine-clad shore south of the town and on the two largest islands off-shore. KATARINA, the closest, is a popular bathing spot. The largest, CRVENI OTOK (Red Island), is actually twin isles linked by a causeway. One, uninhabited, is reserved for naturists. (There's a nudist camp on the mainland, too.) The other has a luxury-hotel complex, including a converted Benedictine monastery. Formerly the Hütteroth family mansion, it boasts 15th-century wall paintings. You can hire a boat to

St. Euphemia's Church dominates charming resort town of Rovinj.

explore the inviting smaller islands such as OTOK LJUBAVI (Isle of Love) and SVETI IVAN (St. John) with its lighthouse.

For romantic ruins, don't miss **Dvigrad** (or Dvograd), a fortified town in the Lim Valley, 20 kilometres from Rovinj. Dvigrad means "two castles", referring to the origin of the town—twin fortified hills that were linked up in the Middle Ages. In 1630, its inhabitants fled to escape an epidemic, and since then only treasure hunters (the people supposedly buried their valuables before leaving) and tourists have come to Dvigrad.

South-east of Rovinj, the ancient town of BALE has interesting medieval architecture. From here, a road first surveyed by Roman engineers cuts straight through pines and scrub for Pula (20 km. from Bale). If you have time, stop off at VODNJAN, another of the fascinating old hill towns of Istria.

Pula
Pop. 60,000

For 2,000 years, Pula has been coveted by every naval power in the eastern Mediterranean. Strategically located at the head of the Adriatic, it stretches around the shore of Istria's largest bay, a natural harbour.

Legend has it that when Jason and Medea made off with the golden fleece, Medea's father sent several ships in pursuit. One crew, too scared to return empty-handed, settled here, presumably to live happily ever after with the local Illyrian maidens. Whether or not they founded Pula, there was certainly a settlement here as early as 500 B.C. The first fortifications were raised on the hill now occupied by the *kaštel*. From there the settlement spread to the shore in concentric circles, a design reflected in the modern city.

The Illyrian capital (near Pula) was sacked by the Romans in 178 B.C. The defeated leaders committed suicide, and Istria became a part of metropolitan Rome.

Judging from the size of its amphitheatre and its highly efficient water supply and drainage systems, Roman Pula had some 30,000 inhabitants. Big landowners built luxurious villas in the area, and their estates produced the wine and olive oil for which Istria was famous even then.

Pula continued to prosper under Byzantine rule. But, after changing hands many times, the city fell to Venice, which allowed it to decline, carrying off its treasures and ruthlessly demolishing Roman monuments for building materials.

Under Austria, Pula saw better days: it was the chief port of the empire. A dockyard and naval arsenal were set up, the railway was brought in and the centre of the city rebuilt. During this period, James Joyce spent some time here teaching English.

A tour of the city should start from its most enduring landmark: the great Roman **arena,** one of the largest and best preserved in existence. Its golden shell has dominated the waterfront since the 1st century. Rumour has it that Emperor Vespasian rebuilt and enlarged the amphitheatre to please his native mistress. The impressive ellipse (436 by 346 feet) could seat 23,000 spectators, but the original stone benches were carted off long

ago by medieval builders. In fact, the Venetians wanted to dismantle the whole arena and re-erect it on the Lido. Thanks to the outraged protests of a pioneer conservationist from Venice, Senator Gabriele Emo, the scheme was dropped.

The four rectangular towers, which contained spiral stair-cases leading to the upper tiers of seats, were part of a complicated waterworks system. On the west tower, you'll see a plaque thanking Senator Emo for saving the amphitheatre.

Gladiator fights and, inevitably, "contests" between wild beasts and Christians took

place in the arena. Underground, a maze of passages leads to the chambers where the "performers" awaited their cue before emerging—perhaps for the last time—into the dazzling sunlight of the arena. These chambers now house Roman artefacts, including olive and wine presses.

Today the arena is used for performances of opera, folk music and the Yugoslav national film festival. It can be visited (depending on daylight conditions) from 8 a.m. to 8 p.m. in summer and correspondingly shorter hours towards winter.

The main street running past the arena leads to the enthusiastically titled Brotherhood and Unity Square *(Trg Bratstva-jedinstva)*, the site of the necropolis mentioned in Dante's *Inferno*. Now the centre of modern Pula, it's flanked by massive city fortifications and by the Roman Hercules' Gate. The double arch nearby *(Porta Gemina, 2nd century A.D.)* now serves as the entrance to the **Archaeological Museum** *(Arheološki muzej)*, noted for extensive prehistoric and Roman collections. On the hillside behind the museum are the remains of a 2nd-century Roman theatre.

At the beginning of May Day Street *(Prvomajska ulica)*, stands a **triumphal arch** erected in the 1st century B.C. to honour three soldier brothers of the Sergi family. A tenacious breed, they seem to have dominated Pula until 1333, when they were banished from the city. This elaborately carved monument with its two pairs of Corinthian columns has been studied and sketched by Michelangelo, Piranesi and Robert Adam.

At the corner of Prvomajska Ulica and the Sergi arch, a plaque on the wall commemorates the fact that James Joyce gave English lessons in the building.

Follow Prvomajska as it circles the *kaštel*. Behind the building at No. 16, you'll see a large mosaic depicting the punishment of mythological Dirce, once the floor of a luxurious Roman villa.

Across a grassed-over bomb site, stands **St. Mary's chapel** *(Sveta Marija Formosa)*. It's all that remains of a 6th-century basilica built by a local boy (Maximian) who later became Archbishop of Ravenna and a saint. Many of its

Pula's impressive Roman arena is now the setting for cultural events.

treasures were carried off to Venice, including the four alabaster columns that now grace the high altar of St. Mark's. The chapel contains 6th-century mosaics and 15th-century frescoes.

Further along Prvomajska, up a steep side street on the right, is a **Franciscan monastery church** of the early 14th century *(Sveti Franjo)*. Its splendid west portal is decorated with carved shells. Hanging over the street is a twin pulpit that catered for the overflow congregations in the days before public-address systems. The 15th-century wooden altarpiece is the finest Venetian Gothic sculpture in Istria. Copies of frescoes from Istrian village churches (the originals being rather inaccessible) are shown in the church cloister along with fragments of medieval stone carvings.

The first thing you'll see in Republic Square *(Trg Republike)* is the perfectly preserved Roman **Temple of Augustus** *(Augustov hram)*, with its tall, slender Corinthian columns. This cool, dignified treasure has come intact through 19 centuries, but the temple of Diana that stood next to it is now only a shadowy outline on the back of the Gothic town hall *(Vijećnica)*. Nearby is the **cathedral.** Once a 6th-century basilica, its interior retains the austere simplicity of Early Christian architecture. The altar, a Roman sarcophagus from the 3rd century, is said to hold the remains of Hungarian King Salomon (11th century).

Crowning the hill in the centre of the city is the **kaštel,** built on the same site as the original Illyrian settlement and the Roman capitol. In the 13th century, the Sergi family pulled down the Roman buildings to make room for their own castle. Retribution for such vandalism followed swiftly. Many of the Sergi were massacred one night in 1271 by a rival political faction; the rest were expelled when Venice took over the city 60 years later.

The present star-shaped castle, designed for the Venetians by a French engineer in the 17th century, now houses the Museum of the National Revolution. Rest here under the trees and contemplate Pula's magnificent harbour. The city's famous shipyard is located on the island of Uljanik, now connected to the mainland.

Thanks to the almost landlocked pattern of the harbour, the surrounding beaches are completely free from pollution. The town beaches, mostly pebble, are at nearby Stoja and Zelenika (buses every half hour). Most tourists stay just outside the city at one of the several holiday "villages". The largest and closest is ZLATNE STIJENE, a complex of hotels and bungalows with its own entertainment and sports facilities.

Surroundings of Pula
A hundred and twenty miles of shoreline within a 10-mile radius of the city, pine woods, fishing villages and a translucent sea make the area ideal for a relaxing sun-filled holiday. Good roads fan out from Pula to several small resorts.

Surrounded by vineyards and orchards, the fishing port of FAŽANA (8 km. to the north) was once a Roman pottery works. One of its three old churches, St. Mary's *(Sveta Marija od Karmela)*, has frescoes in the Gothic style.

Offshore lies the archipelago of **Brioni** *(Brijuni)* where late President Tito used to entertain foreign statesmen. The 14 islands were declared a national park in 1983. Mediterranean and subtropical vegetation — palm trees, bamboo, eucalyptus, cedars and cypresses — characterizes the archipelago, that also houses unique archaeological finds. Deer, mouflons, rabbits and pheasants run free. The island of Vanga, with Tito's white villa, has become a separate memorial area shown to foreign delegations. The largest island, Veliki Brion *(Veli Brijun),* serves as hub of tourist activities, with modern hotel complexes, museums, a zoo and a safari park.

VINKURAN (5 km. south of Pula) has a protected beach in a pine-wood setting. In nearby BANJOLE (a good beach, fishing facilities and ruins of a medieval chapel), POMER (oyster and mussel beds) and other villages in the area, accommodation is available in private houses as well as in camps.

MEDULIN (10 km. to the south-east) was "discovered" by the Romans. They built summer villas near its mile-and-a-half beach. Besides hotels, there are well-equipped, beautifully located naturist and camping sites.

PREMANTURA (12 km. south of Pula, on the Kamenjak promontory) is famous for its shellfish. There are several campsites and both rock and pebble beaches. From here, you can take a walk to CAPE KAMENJAK, the southernmost point of Istria.

Istria's East Coast

From Pula, the 102-kilometre road to Rijeka winds inland through wild and changing scenery. At BARBAN (28 km. from Pula), a fortified medieval town with city gates and a couple of interesting old churches, the road goes down into the Raša river valley. From here the river flows southward into the fjordlike Bay of Raša, actually a sunken valley. Since it marked the frontier of imperial Rome, the Raša was regarded for centuries as the boundary between Istria and Dalmatia. Crossing the river, you unexpectedly enter mining country.

Hilltop LABIN (15 km. from Barban), undermined by a honeycomb of coal galleries, seems doomed to a literal decline and fall. Many of its fine buildings, dating from the 14th to the 18th century, have cracked. Almost all the inhabitants of the old town have been evacuated to the modern mining settlement of Podlabin below, leaving the squares and quaint narrow streets of Labin to the sightseer. One of its patrician mansions was the birthplace of the learned Flacius Illyricus, a pupil of Martin Luther and a leading figure of the Reformation. The battle-

ments of the medieval fortifications command a magnificent view of the Kvarner Gulf and the island of Cres.

From a quiet little fishing village, RABAC has developed over the past few years into a leading seaside resort. Delightfully located in a sheltered cove with pebble and sand beaches backed by olive and pine groves, Rabac has a large number of hotels and bungalows and plenty of sports and entertainment.

PLOMIN (14 km. from Labin), a picturesquely deserted ruin, stands at the head of the sea inlet of Plomin Bay. From here the road runs due north, passes the turning to BRESTOVA, the nearest car-ferry port to the islands of Cres and Lošinj, and soon enters the KVARNER RIVIERA. This stretch of coastline at the foot of Mount Učka's steep, wooded slopes is renowned for its year-round mild climate, lush vegetation and string of attractive little resorts culminating in Opatija.

MOŠĆENIČKA DRAGA (20 km. from Plomin) is a fishing village turned resort thanks to a pebble beach a mile and a half long. Either 760 steps or a 3-

The picturesque fishing village of Mošćenička Draga is now a resort.

kilometre paved road lead from the shore to the old settlement of MOŠĆENICE. A tiny walled town, it has several old buildings. MEDVEJA is another little resort, with perhaps the finest pebble beach on the Kvarner Riviera and a large camping site.

The surrounding laurel groves gave LOVRAN its Roman name, Lauriana. The charming old town is reached through the one remaining gate. On the small square stand the Gothic church of St. George *(Sveti Juraj)*, with its 15th-century frescoes, and a house bearing the figures of the saint and dragon over its doorway.

The resort began to develop in the late 19th century when rich Austrians and Hungarians took to wintering here. From Lovran, a long promenade wanders along the pebble and shingle beaches as far as Opatija and Volosko. It passes by the villages of IKA and IČIĆI, now linked by villas and hotels half hidden in palms, oleanders, hibiscus and other sub-tropical plants.

Dedicated hikers will want to scale Mount Učka or at least its lower slopes. Several villages can be reached from Lovran by marked paths in an hour or so.

A resort in the grand manner, **Opatija** (13 km. from Rijeka) trails clouds of 19th-century glory, conjuring up the era when Emperor Franz Joseph visited his mistress here and the cream of Austro-Hungarian society used to saunter along the seafront.

Opatija started as a fishing village named after the medieval abbey of St. James. It developed into a resort over a century ago, when an enterprising Rijeka businessman built the neo-classical Villa Angiolina on the grounds of what is today Prvi Maj Park. What really put the resort on the map was the opening of the Vienna-Rijeka and Budapest-Rijeka railway lines. In 1873, the line was connected to Opatija by tram. As a favourite wintering place of Central European high society, it acquired imposing hotels and opulent villas in every fanciful style known.

Opatija soon earned a reputation as a year-round health resort, thanks to the high mineral content of the sea and the iodine in the air. The annual average of 2,230 hours of sunshine may have had something to do with its success, too.

New hotels built since the war have scarcely altered the town's gracious Edwardian appearance. The life of Isadora Duncan was partly filmed here, since Opatija looks more like the French Riviera in the twenties than the Riviera itself. To complete the illusion, it has a casino and tiny artificial sandy beaches—though swimming is mostly from the rocks and concrete lidos.

Opatija caters for a wide range of tastes—from opera (weekly performances in the open-air theatre by the sea) to motorcycle racing (at nearby Preluk). As a change from swimming, sailing and water-skiing, you can climb or drive up Mount Učka, the source of refreshing summer breezes and a barrier against cold winter winds.

Stroll through Prvi Maj Park, where giant sequoia tower over exotic plants, or follow the seaside promenade to VOLOSKO, a quaint old fishing village.

Skilled woodcarvers from Opatija perpetuate this traditional craft.

Rijeka

Pop. 220,000

Yugoslavia's number-one port and the biggest city on the eastern Adriatic seaboard, Rijeka is probably more visited and less explored than any other town in the region. Thousands of tourists arriving by rail, road, sea and air pass quickly through on the way to their chosen holiday resort. For a city of this size and antiquity—it was the site of the Roman town of Tarsatica—Rijeka has few ancient monuments. An earthquake in 1750, heavy bombing during World War II and various other misfortunes took their toll.

To simplify Rijeka's complicated history: in the 15th century, it developed as a prosperous Austrian port under the Hapsburgs, rivalling Trieste and Venice. Three centuries later, it passed under Hungarian control until World War I—aside from brief periods of Croatian and French rule. Rijeka/Fiume hit the world's headlines in 1919 when Gabriele D'Annunzio and his band of adventurers occupied the city, claiming it for Italy. After four years as a free state, it was annexed by Italy. The arm of the River Rječina known as Dead Channel *(Mrtvi kanal)* marked the state frontiers. It wasn't until 1945 that the city was reunited and became part of Yugoslavia.

Don't imagine you've seen everything when you've covered the busy cosmopolitan waterfront and the two main shopping streets running parallel with it. From the steamer quay *(Obala Jugoslavenske mornarice),* cut through the

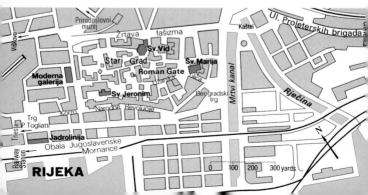

main square *(Narodni trg)* and turn into the Korzo. This will bring you to the clock tower *(Pod uriloj)*, probably 13th century but later much renovated and adorned with the busts of two Austrian emperors. At one time, you had to cross a drawbridge over a moat to enter the **Old Town** *(Stari grad)*. Now there's just an archway in the tower to walk through. This decaying quarter, much the worse for bomb-damage and the ravages of time, is incongruously brightened by an ultra-modern department store. The street ahead is spanned by the Old, or Roman, Gate. To the right, Užarska Street leads to the Baroque cathedral *(Sveta Marija)* with its leaning bell tower.

Quite close by is the church of St. Vitus *(Sveti Vid)*, a circular Baroque edifice containing a famous Gothic wooden crucifix from an earlier church. The bronze hand and stone attached to it commemorate a legend involving swift divine punishment. In 1296, a blasphemous local gambler threw the stone at the cross when his luck deserted him. The ground outside the church immediately swallowed him up, so the story goes, except for the man's hand, which was

The clock tower on Rijeka's main square marks entrance to old town.

cut off and burnt. The dent to the left of the main portal has a less miraculous explanation. It's attributed to a cannonball fired by the British Navy during the Napoleonic wars.

The third church of note in the Old Town is St. Jerome **45**

(*Sveti Jeronim*), a monastery cloister and two medieval chapels with tombs of local nobility and sea captains.

Drive, bus or climb the 536 steps to **Trsat Castle** on the hill for a panorama of this fast-growing industrial city with its shipyards, engineering works, oil refinery and gleaming white apartment buildings that defy gravity, perched along the steep shore of Rijeka Bay. This castle on the site of Illyrian and Roman camps was once owned by the mighty

Old fingers tat busily away; below: *votive offerings in Trsat monastery.*

Frankopan family (see p. 54). Laval Nugent, an Austrian of Anglo-Irish ancestry, bought and adapted the castle to his bizarre tastes early in the 19th century. The little Greek temple he built inside, using Doric columns from Pula, was intended as his mausoleum. It now serves as a bandstand. The rest of the castle has been turned into a restaurant.

On a rise near the castle stands the 15th-century **church of St. Mary** *(Sveta Marija Lauretanska)*, for centuries a popular shrine for pilgrimages. St. Mary's owes its fame to a legend that the house of the Virgin Mary rested here for three years on its miraculous journey from Nazareth to the shrine of Loreto (Italy) in the 13th century. In any case, the painting of the Madonna adorning the high altar was presented to the town by Pope Urban V, perhaps by way of consolation. The adjoining Franciscan monastery houses hundreds of curious votive offerings to St. Mary, mainly from grateful sailors. The quiet old quarter of Trsat is a pleasant place to stop for a cool drink.

For those who want to spend a few days in Rijeka, there are beach-side hotels and campsites at PRELUK and ŽURKOVO.

Excursions from Rijeka

The magnificent alpine-type scenery of the GORSKI KOTAR region begins 15 kilometres north of Rijeka. The Rijeka-Karlovac-Zagreb road twists and turns upwards and Mediterranean scrub soon gives way to dense woods and mountain pastures. PLATAK (3,670 feet above sea level) on the seaward side of MOUNT SNEŽNIK (4,950 feet high) has excellent ski slopes. In late spring, you can ski here in the morning and take a dip in the Adriatic after lunch. Reached by regular and excursion buses from Rijeka, Platak is the starting point for hikes to the peaks of Snežnik (about one hour) and MOUNT VELIKI RISNJAK (two and a half hours).

The Risnjak National Park, covering 14 square miles, is an area of ancient pine forests, limestone caves, swift rivers and artificial lakes. It's renowned for shooting (anything from grouse to bear, provided you have the appropriate licence) and trout-fishing. Further along the Zagreb road are LOKVE with its lake, DELNICE and SKRAD, all centres for hiking, climbing or skiing, depending on the season.

Excursions into Slovenia

Many visitors take time off from the beach to explore the fantastic underground world of the **Postojna Caves** *(Postojnska jama)*, one of the natural wonders of Europe. Situated on the main roads from Koper (62 km.) and Rijeka (72 km.) they have been open to the public for over a century.

The cave system carved out of the limestone by the subterranean river extends for about 13 miles. It includes several smaller caves—Otoška jama, Pivska jama and Črna jama. The visitor to Postojna sees some 3 miles of the most interesting caverns in about two hours, trundling down into the bowels of the earth on a miniature railway, then continuing the tour on foot. Cloaks can be rented at the entrance for those not prepared for the year-round tem-

perature of 48°F. Guides speaking the main European languages provide a commentary during the tour.

The outer chambers were blackened by an ammunition-dump explosion set off by a local partisan during the German occupation. Beyond, you enter an enchanted realm with forests of stalactites and stalagmites in every shape and hue, awe-inspiring chasms, roaring torrents, a "ballroom", and a "concert hall" big enough to hold 10,000 people. An unusual amphibian inhabitant of the caves is the eyeless "man fish" *(Proteus anguineus)*, so-called because of its flesh-coloured skin and tiny hands. A unique prehistoric leftover, it lays eggs at temperatures above 60°F and gives birth to live offspring when it's colder.

An asphalt road leads from the cave to the romantic **Predjamski Grad**, literally "Castle before the Cave". Clinging to the face of a steep cliff, it was built in the 16th century after the older castle, actually inside the huge cave, was deserted. Legend makes it the impregnable fortress of a Slovenian Robin Hood. He and his army of retainers could resist all efforts to starve them out thanks to a secret tunnel connecting the cave with the nearby Vi-

Postojna limestone caves are among Europe's greatest natural wonders.

pava Valley. The castle now houses an interesting archaeological collection, armour and other exhibits.

An attractive excursion for the fairly energetic takes in **Škocjan Caves** *(Škocjanska jame)*, 34 kilometres north-   **49** east of Koper. Though over-shadowed by their bigger and more famous neighbour, Postojna, the Škocjan caves are admired for their wild beauty. They were even mentioned by Pliny and Virgil. Stretching for 3 miles along an underground river, they can be seen in a strenuous hour and a half (guided walks start from the village of MATAVUN at 10 a.m., 1, 3 and 5 p.m. during the summer). Most people feel the need for a sweater. You descend into a gloomy world of mysterious gorges, bridges spanning the foaming river and black lakes, passing into the open as you reach the amazing swallowholes, one with precipitous sides rising almost 600 feet. The austere grandeur of Škocjan will haunt you long after other holiday memories fade.

Most of the magnificent white horses performing in circuses and pulling royal coaches are Lipizzaners, a breed which originated in the stud at **Lipica,** close to the Yugoslav-Italian border. Exceptionally intelligent and long-lived (30 years on the average), they're a cross between Andalusian and local horses. They have been bred here since 1580, when an Austrian archduke founded the stud. The Lipizzaners have al-ways been used in the famous Spanish Riding School of Vienna; their quickness to learn and beautiful action make them ideal for training. Visitors can (for a fee) inspect the stables, see stallions whose pedigree goes back two centuries, watch a dressage display twice daily (11 a.m. and 2.30 p.m., except Saturdays; 3 p.m. on Sundays), and ride themselves (instructors and children's ponies are available). There are few more beautiful sights than a large herd of creamy-white brood-mares with their black foals (it takes several years for them to change colour), returning from the pasture towards sunset.

In a pleasant valley surrounded by the Julian Alps, **Ljubljana** (120 km. from Rijeka) is an attractive blend of old and new: a lively modern town (250,000 inhabitants) with an old quarter beside the river, mostly Baroque in style and Central European in atmosphere.

Start at Prešern Square *(Prešernov trg),* named after

Old Ljubljana has a Central European air; pedigrees of Lipizzaner horses may go back many centuries.

Slovenia's greatest lyric poet, with its Franciscan church. Cross the city landmark of Tromostovlje—three connected bridges spanning the Ljubljanica river—to Stritarjeva Street and the market-place. The big Baroque fountain symbolizing the three rivers of Slovenia is by Francesco Robba, who did much work in the city. Close at hand is the ornate cathedral of St. Nicholas (early 18th century). For a panorama of the Slovenian capital and the Alps beyond, climb up to the medieval fortress (built on Roman foundations) that dominates the city.

The **lake of Bled** (50 km. north of Ljubljana) is something out of a fairy-tale. With a castle perched on a cliff above the lake shore, a tiny island with a church built over a pagan shrine and the towering Julian Alps all round, it would be hard to invent a more romantic spot. No wonder tourists have been coming here for over 200 years: in summer to walk and climb; in winter to skate on the frozen lake and ski on the nearby slopes. There are several very good hotels in the village of Bled and around the lake. A visit to the castle and its historical collection is a "must".

Nearby Italy

What discourages most people from taking a day trip to **Venice*** is the cost: the expensive excursion from Poreč does not include entrance fees, lunch, *vaporetto* and gondola fares. You're guided around the main attractions—St. Mark's, the Doge's Palace, Rialto Bridge and the Murano glass-works. For diligent sightseers, the brief trip is frustrating, especially in July and August when Venice is jammed with tourists. But if all you want is a general impression of this uniquely beautiful city, sign up for the excursion and enjoy a pleasant sea voyage as well.

What attracts hordes of Yugoslavs to **Trieste** (Serbo-Croatian *Trst*) is not ancient monuments but the shops selling shoes, handbags, blue jeans and so on at cheaper prices and in more up-to-date styles than at home. The more discriminating prefer Venice, as Trieste gets "shopped out" at holiday times. The Ponterosso Square open-air market is the place for clothes bargains. Some organized excursions are simply shopping trips; others include a sightseeing tour, taking in the fortress, **San Giusto Cathedral** and **Miramare Castle,** former residence of the ill-fated Emperor Maximilian of Mexico. Prices vary according to the distance and type of excursion.

* For complete information on what to see and do in Venice, take along the Berlitz VENICE TRAVEL GUIDE.

Hans Rudolf Uthoff

Straight out of fairyland, Lake Bled and castle cast their spell. **53**

The Croatian Littoral

From Rijeka, the Adriatic Highway *(Jadranska magistrala)* winds its way down to the Albanian border. The first hundred kilometres or so pass through the Croatian Littoral *(Hrvatsko primorje)*, a narrow stretch of coastline cut off from the interior by the towering Dinaric chain. Before the road opened, the area was little known to tourists.

These stark slopes, once covered with forests, were stripped over the centuries by ship-builders and fuel gatherers. Then erosion turned them into an arid limestone wilderness, bleached in summer by the scorching sun and scoured in winter by the violent north wind, the *bura*. Across the Velebit Channel, the eastern sides of Krk and Rab, also exposed to the *bura*'s fury, look equally inhospitable. No wonder this harsh infertile land bred an extremely tough race of fishermen and seafarers not averse to piracy in the past.

The first town of any size south of Rijeka is BAKAR (16 km.), haven of retired sea captains. A ruined 16th-century castle, the old quarter below it and the 19th-century port at sea level are reminders of past glory.

The sharp turn off the highway for Bakar also connects with the gravel road leading to the fortified medieval settlement of HRELJIN. According to legend, the town was founded by Hercules. Like much of the Croatian Littoral, it belonged in the Middle Ages to the mighty Frankopans of Krk, who dotted the area with their strongholds. The castle stands at the head of Vinodol (wine valley), a long, narrow, fertile strip running parallel to the coast.

Further round the bay, near the village of BAKARAC, you'll see several long ladders jutting out over the waves and maybe a fisherman perched on the end, scanning the sea for tunny (tuna) shoals. Though nowadays a rarity, delicious, grilled fresh tunny steaks are a speciality in this region. When thirsty, try the local sparkling white wine, Bakarska vodica (literally Bakar water).

KRALJEVICA, south of Bakar Bay, has a couple of castles built by the Zrinskis, a powerful family of Croatian nobles who often allied and intermarried with the Frankopans. In the 17th century, the heads of these two families plotted against Austria to gain

Croatian autonomy. The time was ripe. Emperor Leopold had violated all national rights and imposed a rule as tyrannous as the Turks! When promised foreign aid failed to materialize, the two noblemen tried negotiating rather than risking pointless bloodshed. Despite the emperor's solemn

ties and now bears his name.

Tourists stay outside the town at OŠTRO point and the attractive UVALA SCOTT (Scott Cove), a holiday village of modern design. Kraljevica is now linked by a 1,300 yard-long bridge to the island of Krk and Rijeka Airport on its tip.

word, they were both beheaded. Their huge estates were forfeit, the two castles sacked and the illustrious lines of Frankopan and Zrinski extinguished.

Kraljevica's shipyard, formerly under British management, employed Tito as a metalworker in the mid-twen-

CRIKVENICA (24 km. from Bakar) is all parks, promenades and hotels—ornate Austrian or glittering modern. Popular as a bathing and health resort since the turn of the century, it became the "in" place for Yugoslav holidaymakers between the wars. Its balmy climate, long sandy beach and its particularly relaxed atmosphere still attract droves of visitors. Many also stay at the KAČJAK holiday village and the resort of SELCE, in the vicinity, both with good beaches.

The 15th-century Frankopan castle, originally a monastery, stands picturesquely beside the little River Dubračina. For a change of scenery, follow this stream inland to the delightful VINODOL VALLEY.

A trip over to Krk (see p. 62) is no problem: car ferries operate frequently to the village of Šilo, and boat trips are organized to Vrbnik and Malinska.

Generally called just Novi, the ancient town of NOVI VINODOLSKI (9 km. from Crikvenica) has developed into a thriving small resort, spreading along the shore below the medieval settlement. The old town, of which not a great deal survives, is centred around the 13th-century Frankopan castle, much renovated and scarcely recognizable. From the parish

Informality and joviality reign at family gathering; right: Frankopan castle towers over Vinodol Valley.

church of St. Philip and St. James *(Sveti Filip i Jakov)*, there's a magnificent view of the Velebit Channel and the island of Krk. Just as good is the one from the ruins of the 15th-century monastery on the hill above the harbour.

A scenic 5-kilometre trip inland takes you to BRIBIR, formerly a walled Fankopan stronghold.

From Novi to Senj, the Adriatic Highway is edged by the stark grandeur of the Velebit massif, its forbidding aspect in striking contrast to the cheerful green enclaves of Crikvenica and Novi Vinodolski.

For Yugoslavs, the name of **Senj** (23 km. from Novi Vinodolski) conjures up a heroic chapter in their history. In the early 16th century, Senj was a stronghold of the Uskoks, a militant band of refugees from the Turkish territories. Nominally under Austrian rule,

Bathers enjoy unpolluted waters; Pope Leo X tower formed part of Senj's forbidding defence system.

the Uskoks were dedicated to fighting the Ottomans and all who traded with them by land and sea. They soon turned to piracy. In fact, they were aided by a motley collection of foreign buccaneers, including the black sheep of several great English families.

Though numbering only one or two thousand, the daredevil Uskoks with their small, swift craft and adroit seamanship terrorized shipping in the Adriatic. They particularly infuriated Venice, which suffered most from Uskok attacks on its trade routes and on its Istrian ports. Finally they went too far, involving Austria in a two-year war with the Venetian Republic. By the Treaty of Madrid (1617), the Uskoks were disbanded by Austria and resettled inland. Their fleet was burnt and Senj became an Austrian garrison.

The Uskoks' exploits, celebrated in epic poems familiar to every Yugoslav, epitomize the South Slavs' unending struggle for survival and independence. Senj is not a gay resort, but there are some interesting things to see. **Nehaj Fort,** the star attraction, sits on a bluff above the town. Built in the middle of the 16th century as a defence against the Turks, its name *nehaj* ("fear not") sums up the city's defiant attitude. A captured infidel could expect to have his turban nailed to his head—which explains in part the Yugoslav saying: "Beware the hands of Senj…". On a clear day, you can see right to Istria from the battlements of this grim keep, now a museum.

The old quarter of Senj, part of it still walled, merits a stroll. From the harbour follow Potok, the old main street, to the attractive Baroque square *(Ve-*

lika placa). Beside the medieval Frankopan castle (they also owned Senj at one time) stands the imposing Great Gate *(Velika vrata).*

Heavy bombing during World War II scarred Senj badly. Winding streets flanked by ancient houses are punctuated by bombed-out areas. On the Old Square *(Stari trg)* stands a 12th-century cathedral with Baroque touches. Continue on through Gorica, the oldest section of town—a warren of narrow streets unchanged since Uskok times—to the remaining city walls and three medieval towers.

Ferry services operate between Senj and Baška, on the southern tip of Krk, and Lopar in the north of Rab. For both, advance booking for cars is necessary. If you're going to Rab by car, it's better to drive to Jablanac (37 km. south) where the ferries are larger and run more frequently. The sight of the offshore islands, basking like lizards in the green-blue sea, is memorable.

Senj is the nearest coastal town to the **Plitvice Lakes** *(Plitvička jezera),* a celebrated natural wonder. The 84-kilometre drive from Senj, an experience in itself, snakes up to the VRATNIK PASS. In winter the wind is so fierce here, it has

been known to derail trains. At ŽUTA LOKVA, the road branches off eastward to the Plitvice National Park, magnificent unspoilt woodland between the Mala Kapela and Plješevica Mountains.

The big attraction here is the 16 lakes, cascading in innumerable waterfalls one into another. The highest, Prošćansko jezero, is 2,087 feet above sea level; and the lowest, Novakovića brod, 1,600 feet. The lake water then thunders over the Sastavci Falls into the River Korana. Kozjak, the largest lake, has several attractive hotels, bungalows and a campsite on its wooded shores. Bathing, boating and troutfishing (with a permit) are allowed in some areas. Amateur geologists will have a marvellous time inspecting rare travertine formations, numerous caves and other natural phenomena. The entrance ticket comes with a free map indicating various walks and vantage points.

Water from Plitvice's 16 interconnecting lakes cascades down successive falls on way to sea.

The Kvarner Islands

Tourists took a long time to "discover" the Kvarner Islands, except for Lošinj. Perhaps they were deterred by the forbidding, barren shoreline or were loath to leave the charms of Opatija and Crikvenica. Whatever the reason, the islands remained off the beaten track and have kept their authentic atmosphere, local customs and countryside intact.

You don't have to rough it in order to bask on their splendid beaches or explore their fascinating old towns. An international airport, frequent ship and car-ferry services, new roads and modern hotels ensure swift travel and every comfort.

Though geographers lump the Kvarner Islands together, each of them has a character and history of its own.

Krk
Pop. 15,000
Pronounced something like the Scottish *kirk,* the word's no printing error. As usual along the Adriatic, the island and its main town bear the same name. Though tourists may have been slow to appreciate the attractions of Yugoslavia's largest island, it obviously

Handicrafts are important small industry in Yugoslavia; left: Krk, medieval centre of Croat culture.

The island had its heyday in the early Middle Ages, when the lords of Krk, the Frankopans (see p. 54), controlled the Croatian Littoral, paying only nominal homage to Venice and the Hungaro-Croatian kings. In 1480, family discord led one brother to cede Venice his right to Krk, leaving the Frankopans only their mainland possessions. During the centuries of Venetian rule, the island's importance and prosperity steadily declined. Always a strong centre of Croat culture, Krk boasts some of the oldest inscriptions in the ancient glagolitic alphabet, the first form of writing used by the Slavs.

Krk town (about 30 km. from the airport) now has only 1,300 inhabitants, less than a tenth of the number in Roman and medieval times. Its massive fortifications and the fine old buildings lining its narrow cobbled streets testify to past pride and prosperity.

From the waterfront, pass through the Small Gate *(Mala vrata)* and along an inner street *(Ulica Jugoslavenske armije)* to the most interesting cluster of medieval buildings on the North Croatian coast. On your right, the long, low Bishop's Palace and the former Frankopan castle rise sheer

suited some early settlers. Traces of Stone Age men have been found in caves near Baška and Vrbnik. With two small lakes and a river, Krk has no shortage of fresh water. Although the north-eastern shore, whipped by the north wind, is bare limestone rock, the rest is mostly green and fertile. Farming by time-honoured methods and fishing remain the chief occupations.

63

above the waves. On the left, a 12th-century **cathedral,** built over Roman baths and a 5th-century basilica, is famous for a Gothic silver screen showing the Madonna in glory and the beautifully carved capitals of its Roman pillars. Through a trap-door in a side chapel, you can see a mosaic floor from the baths. A narrow, arched passageway links the cathedral to the curious double-decker **basilica of St. Quirinus.** The simple 10th-century lower level, long a wine cellar, was restored in 1963. The Romanesque upper church, built a hundred years later, spans the passageway. You enter it through the bell tower, to which an incongruous onion dome has been added. The square tower across the street is 12th century, the oldest part of the *kaštel.* From the 16th-century round tower you have views of the sea and city. The rest of the castle is a roofless shell laid out as the bishop's garden, next to his palace.

South across the bay lies PUNAT, now more populous than its historical neighbour. Guarding the entrance to an almost enclosed bay, this is a lively place with good bathing, hotels, caravan (trailer) and naturist camps. Colourful fishermen's festivals attract many visitors. The picturesque islet of KOŠLJUN is only a five-minute trip by motor-boat. See the 16th-century Franciscan monastery church and the cloisters housing a museum, with exhibits ranging from Roman pottery and local costumes to stuffed animal freaks.

On the southern tip of Krk, on a wide bay edged by a long sand and pebble beach and backed by a fertile valley is the quaint village of BAŠKA. No wonder prehistoric man

Swimming pools and shaded walks provide welcome refuge from sun.

and then the Romans chose to settle in this idyllic spot. The whole area is scattered with archaeological relics and tiny churches, some dating back to the 9th century. Though tourist establishments are beginning to spread west of the old town along the shore, this is still a quiet and unspoilt place for those who want to unwind and enjoy the sea and sun.

VRBNIK, the only east coast settlement of any size, has defied all comers from its clifftop for 800 years. More an excursion place than a resort, this Frankopan citadel has preserved little of its defence system but has several interesting old buildings. Now that pirates and marauding fleets no longer threaten, cottages have spread out down the steep hillside to the pebble cove below. The vineyards of Vrbnik are celebrated for Zlahtina, the "golden" wine.

The north-west coast is the island's fastest-growing tourist region. The pleasant little resort of MALINSKA is now outshone by its offshoot, a glamourous hotel-village called HALUDOVO. Intended mainly for the well-heeled holiday-maker, this resort has first-class hotels, a newly built "fishing village" and luxury villas, all nicely landscaped. A delightful walk follows the shore to NJIVICE, an authentic fishing village several kilometres further north. However, with its sandy beach and wooded surroundings, this, too, is being developed for tourism.

OMIŠALJ, another hilltop stronghold of the Frankopans, **65**

is the northernmost settlement on Krk. Its medieval quarter, little changed over the years, centres on the main square and Romanesque church of St. Mary. Dubac Square nearby offers a marvellous panorama of Omišalj Bay and the coastline as far as northern Istria.

Rab

Pop. 8,500

Sheltered by long, steep limestone ridges, most of Rab island enjoys a mild and exceptionally sunny climate (2,500 hours of sunshine a year). Though the highlands are bleak, the rest of Rab is delight-

fully green: covered with vineyards, olive groves, wheatfields and woods, with over 300 fresh-water springs.

Settled successively by the Illyrians, Greeks and Romans, during the Middle Ages it bounced back and forth between Venice and the Croatian kingdom. Venice finally won out, but Rab enjoyed considerable autonomy. In 1920, after more than a century of Austrian rule, it became part of Yugoslavia.

With its four campaniles rising above the narrow promontory, the **town of Rab** seems like a graceful four-masted schooner sailing out to sea. Comparable to Dubrovnik, though on a much smaller scale, the old part of the town lies between the colourful harbour and St. Euphemia Bay *(Uvala Sveta Fumija)*. Strolling its flagstone streets is like stepping back to a more gracious and leisurely age. To really appreciate Rab requires time to "stand and stare". The glowing cream-coloured stone, deep blue sky, brilliant oleanders are as harmonious as the setting.

The three principal streets run parallel, one above the other. The middle one is the main shopping street. The highest *(Ulica Rade Koncara)* along the ridge of the promontory, has no less than six churches. The pink-and-white striped façade near the end of the street belongs to the former **Cathedral of St. Mary Major** *(Sveta Marija Velika)*. An outstanding example of a small Romanesque basilica, it was consecrated by Pope Alexander III in 1177. The expressive Gothic *Pietà* (1514) over the doorway, the 15th-century choir stalls and a six-sided canopy with 9th-century stone-carving are among the treasures to be seen here. Close by stands the tallest (90 feet) and most beautiful of the city's four bell towers. Dating from the 12th century, it ranks among the finest Romanesque campaniles to be seen. The energetic will enjoy the superb views from the top.

Just below the cathedral, you enter the warren of lanes and passageways known as Kaldanac, the most ancient part of Rab. Semi-deserted since the 15th century, it was actually walled off to keep a plague epidemic from spreading. The

Rooftops of Rab, one of Kvarner Islands' sunniest spots; above: a face reflects a lifetime of hard toil.

bricked-up windows and doorways can still be seen.

The New Town *(Novi grad)* was, in fact, built between the 14th and 17th centuries. The most recent part, Varoš, has most of the hotels. Lovely Komrčar Park with its gigantic crooked pines is set above St. Euphemia Bay, where bathers splash in the crystal-clear water. Lively and gay in summer, Rab has excellent, privately owned fish restaurants and lots of nightlife.

If you haven't had your fill of sea and sand, head for the quiet fishing village of LOPAR, 13 kilometres north of Rab town (there's a bus service). The finest of several lovely beaches on the island is the crescent-shaped Paradise Beach *(Rajska plaža)*, more than a mile of golden sand with a gently sloping beach. The hotel complex beside it is named after San Marino, the founder of the postage-stamp republic. According to legend, he was a native of Lopar.

The road from Rab town to Kampor goes past the old monastery of St. Euphemia and the impressive Slav Cemetery *(Slovensko groblje)*. This memorial commemorates 4,500 victims of an Italian concentration camp. Both sites are within walking distance of Rab.

Pine, cypress and cork oak cover the KALIFRONT peninsula. Footpaths through these woods lead to many secluded coves where you can sunbathe and swim in complete privacy.

The small resort of BANJOL, south of Rab harbour, has several hotels and fine sandy beaches, while BARBAT, on the road to the car ferry at Pudarica, is noted for its lobsters. A popular boat trip from Rab takes you to the village of LUN on the lace-making island of Pag.

Cres and Lošinj

Pop. 4,000 and 8,500

Once connected by a narrow strip of land, later separated by a canal and now reunited by a bridge, Cres and Lošinj are hardly the Siamese twins you might imagine. Cres, second largest of the Adriatic islands in area, but with a population of only 4,000, is mostly arid limestone hills. Lošinj, on the other hand, the smallest of the Kvarner's Big Four, has luxuriant vegetation and more than twice as many inhabitants.

One of the most hair-raising motoring experiences imaginable is the 83-kilometre route from the car ferry at Porozina in northern Cres to the town of Veli Lošinj way down south. At one point, near Porozina, you drive along the top of a narrow ridge with a dizzying 1,000-foot drop to the sea on either side. This road, linking up almost all the settlements previously dependent on boat services, has given a great boost to tourism.

The fertile area around the **town of Cres** comes as a delightful surprise after so much desolate rock. An old fishing port with several hotels, it was Crespa to the Romans and Cherso to the Venetians, who ruled it for centuries. In the spacious main square *(Narodni trg)* leading off the harbour are a 15th-century loggia, the old town hall and a 16th-century clock tower. Going through the main town gate in the tower, you'll find the closely packed streets typical of the medieval walled cities in this region formerly infested with pirates. Straight ahead, hemmed in by old houses, stand the campanile and

Veli Lošinj – formerly a Venetian bastion against the Uskok pirates.

church of St. Mary of the Snows *(Majka Božja Sniježne)*, 15th century. The tiny church of Sveti Sidar in the maze of streets on the right has a remarkable wooden statue of St. Isidore. A section of the defence walls and two other gates mark the limits of the town. Just outside is the Gothic church of the **Franciscan monastery** (14th–15th century) and its two cloisters.

To the south, a large lake, Vransko jezero, is the only source of fresh water on Cres, which has no streams. It supplies both Cres town and Mali Lošinj. For obvious reasons, you're not allowed to swim in it.

Coming upon **Osor** on the straits separating Cres and Lošinj, you'd never guess that this village of scarcely 100 inhabitants was once a Roman city of 20,000. Under Byzantine rule and later the Croatian kings, it ranked as the leading town of both islands. When the Venetians stopped using the narrow, Roman canal and moved their administration to the town of Cres in the 15th century, Osor was abandoned to the ravages of the Uskok pirates and malaria epidemics. The early Renaissance cathedral, adorned with Italian paintings, gives some indication of the past glory of Osor. So do the remains of the extensive city walls. The surrounding area is a happy digging ground for archaeologists. Sir Richard Burton, a Victorian explorer and celebrity, unearthed some of the artefacts on view in the local museum.

Over the bridge and you're in Lošinj. Almost two islands in itself, the southern part is the tourist mecca. Its superb coastline and climate—mild winters and 2,580 hours of sun annually—began attracting holiday-makers and asthma sufferers a century ago. At that time, it was under Austrian rule. MALI LOŠINJ then had six large shipyards and a fleet of 150 ships. Today, shipbuilding takes second place to tourism. With colourfully painted shops and cafés around the harbour and up the hill, this is a cheerful, animated resort.

The majority of its hotels (one has a casino) are scattered among the pine woods of ČIKAT peninsula. Bathing is mostly from pebble beaches and flat rocks. The indented shoreline and clear water make Mali Lošinj a centre for underwater fishing (an international contest is held here every January 1). Climb to the ruins of the Venetian fortifications on the hill above town for views of the islands and Kvarner Gulf.

South of Mali (small) Lošinj lies its "big" neighbour, VELI LOŠINJ, a misnomer today since it has a population of only 1,000. An attractive place, built around a narrow inlet of the sea and half buried in subtropical vegetation, it has several old buildings, including the 15th-century Uskok Tower, raised by the Venetians against the buccaneers. The village of ROVENSKA in the next cove has a good pebble beach. Naturists will find several very nice camps in southern Lošinj.

If you feel like running away from civilization or just getting a breath of sea air, take an all-day boat trip from Mali Lošinj to the islands of OLIB, SILBA and ILOVIK. Each of them has one tiny village and wonderful deserted beaches. And try the local wine and cheese. Olib has an unusual monument marking the liberation of its peasantry from serfdom only 75 years ago. The only accommodation here is in private homes.

A shorter trip will take you to the island of SUSAK, entirely composed of sand. Geologists are still arguing about how it got there. Covered with terraced vineyards, it's famous for its wine and bright mini-skirted folk costumes.

What to Do

Folklore

If you arrive expecting a land of colourfully garbed peasants, you'll be disappointed. In fact, nowadays the nearest thing to a national costume is the ubiquitous blue jeans. At traditional festivals—"fishermen's days", village fairs and the like—you'll often see the attractive traditional dress, which in any case has always been reserved for holidays. For work a simpler version was worn (and still is in remote areas). The most extraordinary costume is the frilly, multicoloured, multi-layered, miniskirts worn by the women of the tiny island of Susak.

You can get a glimpse of the astonishing range of Yugoslav national costumes—alpine to oriental in style—by attending one of the many folk-song and dance concerts organized in all resorts. The best companies give exciting if stylized performances, from Slovenian polkas to Albanian sword-dances. The costumes are magnificent. Even less renowned local groups usually provide a gay evening's entertainment.

Yugoslavs are very attached to their old folk songs, and on any festive occasion they will leap up to link arms in an energetic *kolo* dance. Along the coast, pop groups in hotels and restaurants often play up-dated arrangements of lively Dalmatian folk songs, some rather Italian in character. The original versions can often be heard when a group of Dalmatian men get together by the harbour or round a café table. They rightly pride themselves on their close-harmony singing.

Istrian music, accompanied by the bagpipe, sounds more archaic, similar to the harsher, less melodious music of the Dinaric hinterland.

Festivals

Carnivals and saints' days, wine and fishing festivals are celebrated all along the coast.

The Yugoslav Folklore Festival is held in July in the Slovenian seaside resorts (Portorož, Koper, Izola, Piran and Ankaran). Leading folk-song and dance companies of Yugoslavia are featured.

Opatija, July and August, opera and ballet festival.

Senj, beginning of August, traditional summer carnival and parade.

Novi Vinodolski, beginning

of August, folklore week with ancient customs of the region.

Punat (Krk), second Saturday in August, Punat Night, fishing and folklore.

Baška (Krk), August, Fishermen's Day festival.

Opatija-Preluk, September, Yugoslav Grand Prix speedway racing.

Poreč, second week of September, Tourist Week, contests and entertainment.

Rijeka, September, rowing regatta.

Buje, September, grape-harvest festival.

Kastav near Opatija, beginning of October, White Week, traditional tasting of new wine.

Svetvinčenat (near Pula), mid-October, day of Istrian music, folklore and new wine.

Lovran, October, chestnut-picking week with festivities *(Marunada)*.

Mali Lošinj, around New Year's Day, international underwater fishing contest.

Films

Even the small towns have cinemas. In most places the films are shown outdoors on summer nights; the natural air-conditioning, unlike indoor ventilation, always works. Most of the films are foreign. They're shown with the original soundtrack, be it English, French or Italian. Subtitles translate into one of the Yugoslavian languages.

Programmes are not continuous; each showing is a separate sitting. Seats are generally numbered (*red* = row; *levo* = left; *desno* = right). In small towns there are intermissions for changing reels.

Nightlife

Up and down the coast, excitement turns up in unexpected places. A fishing village may be hiding a discotheque as raucous as one could desire. A luxury hotel apparently inhabited only by prim museum-lovers may run a lively nightclub—floor show, dancing and all. Some of the bigger hotels have gambling casinos to round out the glamour. Roulette, chemin de fer, blackjack, craps and slot machines compete for your investment. The sign *Bar* indicates a nightclub; bars are called *bife*.

Travel agencies operate night cruises aboard floating

dance palaces plying the Adriatic, with calls at a fishermen's village for more dancing and drinking.

Pop-music, folk-music and other concerts, like all the events of interest to tourists, are prominently advertised, often in English and German as well. During July and August, the basilica in Poreč provides a magnificent setting for weekly concerts of classical music.

Galleries and Museums

In Istria, they are small and local in character: places to pop into for half an hour rather than browse all day. Still, they give an insight into the life of the area. The best paintings are usually found in churches and monasteries.

Koper, Art and History Museum in Baroque Belgramoni-Tacco Palace: old masters and Roman sculptures.

Pazin, the museum in the ancient castle illustrates Istrian way of life.

Piran, the town museum has fine old model ships, archaeological finds, paintings and room commemorating the town's favourite son, violinist Giuseppe Tartini.

Poreč, the town museum has Bronze Age and Etruscan pottery and Roman mosaics.

Exhibits in Pula's museum include many relics of town's Roman past.

Portorož, Forma Viva modern sculpture display in Seća Park.

Pula, Archaeological Museum has Illyrian and Roman collections. Franciscan monastery: stone-carving and copies of medieval frescoes from Istrian churches.

Punat (Krk), folk costumes in the Franciscan monastery on the isle of Košljun.

Rab, St. Justina's church holds religious art and early manuscripts, including musical scores.

Rijeka, Maritime and History Museum, an impressive neo-classical edifice with some original furnishings; model **75**

ships. Modern Art Gallery, 19th- and 20th-century Yugoslav artists.

Rovinj, notable paintings in the town museum, old masters and modern Yugoslav.

Senj, Nehaj Fort has old weapons and ethnological exhibits.

For Children

Most children are very happy with seaside activities—swimming, collecting seashells and intriguing stones and constructing sand castles. The larger hotels have their own playgrounds and children's paddling pools, table tennis or minigolf.

Boat rides provide an adventurous change of pace, either the local ferries or half-day cruises. Don't forget to take extra precautions against sunburn on these trips.

Rijeka, Piran and Rovinj have aquariums.

The folklore shows, with the kaleidoscope of costumes, rhythms and tunes, ought to please all but the smallest children.

View from a Venetian window: dawdling child and lace vendor.

Shopping

Buying trinkets can be one of the amusing features of a foreign holiday. As elsewhere, the Adriatic coast sells a few white elephants among the bargains. One tourist's prize catch is another's dust-catcher.

As for haggling over prices, this is a rare pursuit in Yugoslavia these days. It's almost entirely confined to outdoor markets where craftsmen sell their own work. All the major shops and most of the minor ones are socially owned with fixed prices marked on the goods. It would be futile to haggle in any of these shops

and quite possibly offensive. But street pedlars and the owners of small handicraft shops may accept your challenge to negotiate the price.

Even if you've no interest in buying souvenirs, you'll enjoy browsing through the shops for their cross-section of regional crafts. In the non-tourist shops you can see how and what the Yugoslavs buy. Check on local fashions and prices. The food shops and supermarkets, too, provide another view of the standard of living—and its cost.

Shopping hours follow the typical Mediterranean pattern —early morning to early evening with a long break during the heat of the afternoon. Typically, shops stay open from about 8 a.m. to noon, closing for lunch and siesta and reopening at leisure from 5 to 8 p.m. However, a certain number of shops—mostly supermarkets—remain open all day without a break. These anti-siesta establishments are marked *non-stop*.

Rijeka is the largest commercial centre of the northern coast, with several modern department stores. Pula, Koper and Poreč are also good for shopping. However, in other resorts and even in the more obscure villages you may find 77

FILIGRAN

shops selling items not to be found elsewhere.

Here are some items to look for. Knowledgeable travellers consider them either relatively cheap in Yugoslavia or unique —and sometimes both.

Copper ware, including Turkish-style coffee grinders, pots and cups, exotic and inexpensive.

Crystal. Imaginative and relatively inexpensive, worth

Traditional Yugoslav handcrafted products include filigree jewelry and rugs; fresh herbs may make more piquant holiday souvenirs.

keeping an eye out for special pieces.

Dolls. Collectors can stock up on the national costumes of all the republics of Yugoslavia.

Embroidery ranges from handkerchiefs to lavishly decorated skirts and blouses.

Footwear, perhaps made before your eyes, sometimes in the bargain category.

Gramophone records are a bargain—folk-music, the classics or a Balkan version of a pop song.

Lace, like embroidery, is a traditional skill in parts of Yugoslavia.

Leather goods, such as wallets, luggage, handbags, need a close look and comparative pricing.

Postage stamps make cheap, thoughtful gifts for collectors on your list.

Posters and prints. Another money-saving idea; look for cheap but good reproductions of charming contemporary Yugoslavian art.

Pottery. For instance, hand-painted plates in bright colours and one-of-a-kind designs to brighten your home.

Rugs. Like much of the handwork on sale along the coast, these originate in less sophisticated inland areas; look for original hand-loomed patterns.

Silver filigree jewelry is made in traditional designs by Moslem craftsmen. The shops are privately owned so you could try a bit of discreet bargaining.

Spirits. Relatively cheap, often impressively packaged gifts. Consider *maraskino* (morello-cherry flavour) and *šljivovica,* the plum brandy of renown.

Wood carving. Salad sets, statuettes, flutes, nutcrackers, cigarette boxes, knickknacks, mass-produced by hand. Ornate, decorative and useful.

Woven fabrics. Tablecloths, dress material, shoulder bags, in typical Yugoslavian patterns.

Sports and Other Activities

For the tourist seeking vigorous exercise or just a paddle in unpolluted water, the shores of the Adriatic fill the bill for healthful outdoor recreation.

rays. Wear a hat at midday. You can buy suntan lotion on the spot.

Swimming is the most basic way of enjoying the placid sea along the Yugoslav coast. Rocky coves, pebble beaches, manmade embankments and sandy expanses alternate, though the last are not numer-

But whatever your sport, watch out for too much sun. If you're shivering and shrivelled from sunburn, you won't enjoy your holiday very much. An hour's excess exposure on opening day is quite enough to spoil everything. Do nothing drastic until your skin has become accustomed to the powerful

Adriatic shore offers water sports for all tastes, from slapstick...

ous. Depending on the locale, the facilities may range from zero, or perhaps an elementary shower, to parasols and pampering bar service on the beaches of luxury hotels.

Snorkelling gives the swimmer an undistorted, uninterrupted view of the submarine world. Sporting-goods shops in the towns sell masks, breathing tubes and flippers but they're expensive. Because of the exceptional transparency of the Adriatic and the proliferation of fish, these are splendid waters for the undersea fan.

Scuba diving is very tightly controlled. You need a permit from the local authorities in charge of internal affairs. A travel agency can get this for you. Underwater fishing with diving equipment is forbidden. In the northern Adriatic region, underwater activity is restricted in some areas around Pula, around the islands of Grgur and Goli, in part of Lošinj and around the islands of Silba, Molat and Premuda. Check on this locally.

Boating. If you're visiting Yugoslavia aboard your own yacht, you must apply for a sailing permit at your first port of call. Service facilities may be found in ports big and small. If you'd like to hire a yacht, this, too, can be arranged. A professional crew is optional. At certain beaches you can hire small sailing-boats. Rowing-boats and small motor-boats are also available on an hourly basis.

Water-ski instruction and facilities are available at many resorts. Poreč even offers kite-skiing.

...to snorkelling or more serious scuba diving in the pellucid sea.

A final seaside sport, **fishing**; the number of regulations seems to equal the number of species waiting to take your hook. For the latest instructions, check with the local authorities when you reach your resort. Equipment may be bought in sporting-goods shops in the towns. Incidentally, after **81** you've gone through the formalities, you may find your daily catch is restricted to 5.5 kilograms (12 pounds). Hardly a morning's work, to hear some anglers tell it.

Sports Ashore

Tennis isn't a major sport in Yugoslavia but courts do exist at certain hotels as well as tennis clubs.

Golf hasn't come to the area because of the rocky terrain. In the absence of a course of any description, fans will have to make do with **minigolf,** a common enough diversion around the hotel circuit.

Mountain climbing attracts many enthusiasts to the Gorski Kotar region, just north of Rijeka, and Mount Učka, above the Opatija Riviera. Don't underestimate the midday sun at high altitudes.

Game shooting. Istria is noted for its feathered game and the Gorski Kotar region for larger prey. But it's a pretty expensive sport: you have to pay for what you kill.

Riding. In some places you can hire horses by the hour, but Lipica is the centre for equestrian holidays. An obliging peasant may let the youngsters have a go on his donkey.

If you play, don't hesitate to seek a game; chess is a national passion.

Skiing. In the very early spring, you could conceivably alternate between the sunny seaside and the snowy slopes. While your coastal resort may back on to a snow-topped mountain, the nearest real ski centre is probably many miles away. The best-run ski resorts are all in the north, in Slovenia, which borders on ski-conscious Austria. Package-tour companies run winter sports holidays from Britain to sophisticated Yugoslavian resorts such as Bled and Bohinj.

Spectator Sports

Football. Soccer is a serious pursuit in Yugoslavia though the principal matches are held outside the tourist season. You may stumble onto less formal warm-ups locally.

Water-polo. Each Adriatic village seems to field a team ready to drown for local honour. An exciting game to watch when spirits reach flood tide.

Other Pursuits

Bowling alleys have been opened in half a dozen major tourist hotels along the northern coast.

Table-tennis is very widely available.

Chess is more of a major national sport than in most Western countries. If you can play, it's a good way to make contact with the Yugoslavs.

Flora and Fauna

Luxuriant subtropical plants, aromatic scrub and pine forests grow only a few miles apart in Istria. Cherry, laurel and sweet chestnut trees spill down the slopes of Mount Učka while **83** palms, oleander and bougain-villea line the shore below.

In Opatija's main park, a real botanical garden, giant sequoia tower over magnolia and pampered exotic bushes. Pines scent the air and provide welcome midday shade along the western coast.

Inland, a pair of white oxen yoked to a cart may surprise you around a bend. Their curved horns are impressive. Everywhere, the small, brown donkeys patiently trudge along with their burdens.

The Adriatic Sea is home to hundreds of species—enchant-ing or gruesome, delicious or dangerous. Fishermen will of-ten meet eel, perch, bass and mullet. The open sea is rich in sardine, mackerel and tunny (tuna). Local menus confirm the proximity of squid, mussels and lobster.

Cautious swimmers will be relieved to learn that, while sharks do appear in the Adria-tic, the blue or man-eating monsters are exceedingly rare.

You'll find few jelly fish around, but watch out for the spiny, black sea urchins on rocky beaches. A pair of plastic sandals will protect your feet.

Wining and Dining

Good food stands high on the Yugoslavs' list of priorities, so whether you eat to live or live to eat, you can set about holi-day wining and dining with confidence and pleasurable an-ticipation.

Seafood and pasta have been the mainstay of Adriatic cui-sine for generations. Unfortu-nately, the sea is becoming less bountiful and, except in out-of-the-way corners, peak-season demand for freshly netted fish far exceeds the avail-able supply. But don't worry. Diversity of culture produces diversity of cookery, and the specialities of other regions are well established up and down the coast. Just follow your nose, and you'll soon find a hooded charcoal grill with sizzling shishkebabs, spitted lamb or sucking pig. And to wash these delicacies down, a wide assortment of wines, many first-class and generally inexpensive.

But trying some of these exotic and tasty specialities often means venturing beyond the hotel dining-room with its multilingual menus and "inter-national" cuisine. Where to go? We make no recommenda-tions, award no stars, whisper no tips. Last year's discovery may turn into this season's disappointment. Even at best, there's no accounting for taste. But we'll tell you what you ought to know before you decide where to dine and what to look for once you're glancing at the bill of fare.

Remember that the fanciest décor doesn't necessarily guarantee the best food. A modest, privately owned *gostiona* can often outdo the plushest establishment when it comes to local specialities. First, a rundown of the various types of eating places:

Bife: this is the way the Yugoslavs write *buffet*—a snack bar serving all kinds of drinks, sandwiches, cold cuts and sometimes hot meals.

Ekspres restoran: a bit short on atmosphere as a rule—a rough-and-ready, self-service café; limited menu but good for your budget.

Kafana: a term covering everything from a coffee-and-cake shop in a large hotel to a full-scale restaurant; alcoholic drinks available in any case.

Mlečni restoran: a dairy shop which deals in light meals, pancakes, pastry, yoghurt, milk and even coffee.

Gostiona: a village inn or smaller restaurant, often privately owned; home-cooked,

When hunger strikes, follow your nose to the sizzling shishkebab.

wholesome food, prepared and served by the proprietor and his family. Some have rooms to let.

Restoran: just about any restaurant from the humble to the elegant.

Slastičarna: ice-cream parlour plus cake-shop serving espresso coffee, fruit juices, dozens of flavours of ice-cream, as well as oriental pastries for the sweet-toothed.

Konoba: a wine cellar where you can enjoy local wine in gay ceramic jugs and a snack. **85**

Eating Habits

Breakfast *(doručak)* is not a big production in Yugoslavia. In tourist hotels ham-and-egg breakfasts may be obtained, but generally it's a matter of coffee or tea, rolls or bread, butter and jam with perhaps a soft-boiled egg or piece of cheese on the side. Breakfast

Miješano meso, *one of the many delicious Yugoslavian specialities.*

coffee *(bijela kafa—*white coffee) is generally made with a coffee substitute. If you prefer, you can always bring a jar of instant coffee to the breakfast table and ask for hot water *(topla voda)* or hot milk *(toplo mlijeko).* Most seaside hotels are used to this practice; some even supply the instant coffee. If you sit at the same place for all meals, you can probably leave the jar on the table (the same applies to unfinished bottles of wine or other drinks). And tea drinkers who find the brew too weak for their taste, can bring along some extra tea bags and pop one in to strengthen the mixture, then ask for cold milk *(hladno mlijeko).*

In mid-morning, you may come upon a café where the locals drop in for a second breakfast *(marenda),* often in the form of a goulash or fish stew *(brodet).* This naturally leads to a glass of wine, and that's the end of your sightseeing. On the other hand, "When in Rome…"

The main meal of the day is lunch *(ručak)* though a hefty dinner *(večera)* also figures in the plan. A principal difference between the two meals is that soup tends to be replaced by a cold first course in the evening.

Meal times depend on the level of sophistication of the clientele. In fishing villages, for instance, dinner is over early. Elsewhere it could run till 10 or 11 p.m. In hotels, breakfast is served from about 7 to 9 a.m., lunch from noon to 2 p.m. and dinner from 7 to 9.

Most restaurants do not add a service charge to bills. If they do, it should be noted on the menu. Leaving a tip is customary: 5-10 per cent would be normal. Don't feel shy about checking a bill if it's more than you expected. By law, prices must be listed on the menu or, in smaller restaurants, posted.

Some restaurants offer fixed-price menus *(turistički meni)*, usually three courses without wine and a limited choice.

A menu is a *jelovnik,* and here are some of the treats to look for:*

Appetizers

Istarski or *Dalmatinski pršut:* smoked ham, a distinctive delicacy of the coast, justly famous for its subtle flavour.

Gavrilovićeva salama: a tangy salami reminiscent of the best from Italy.

Kajmak: made with the skin of scalded milk, it has a unique flavour and cheesy texture.

Soups

Categorized either as *juha,* a broth, or *čorba* (a thick soup), they come in many varieties and may be grouped together as *juha.*

Dining in a cool, fragrant court-yard makes any meal seem special.

Fish and Shellfish

According to an old saying, the Adriatic can produce a different kind of fish for every day in the year. Only a fraction ever appear on the table. Mackerel and sardines, grilled or fried, are the most commonly served. For more distinguished fare, choose bass, dentex or bream, grilled slowly over coals. Pungent fish stews *(brodet)*, often served with *palenta*, a purée of maize (cornmeal), are native to the region, recipes varying from village to village. Another way of preparing fish is *lešo* (poached).

Shellfish—lobster, or more often crab, oysters, shrimp, mussels—though delicious, are rather expensive. Boiled lobster, or crab, usually served cold with mayonnaise, is a delicacy. Mussels, steamed open or tossed in a *rizoto* (rice dish), are another speciality.

Meat Dishes

Charcoal-grilled meat *(roštilj)* is perhaps the most ubiquitous item on Yugoslav menus. The best is usually to be found in restaurants, large or small, with an outdoor barbecue. Most popular as a supper dish, *roštilj* comes in all shapes and sizes, invariably served with chopped raw onion and often accompanied by a salad. Among them:

Ćevapčići: small sausage-shaped meat rolls (beef or beef-pork mixture); ten is the usual portion.

Pljeskavica: a large hamburger steak. If you don't like spicy food, say *"ne ljuto"* ("not hot") when ordering.

Ražnjići: skewered chunks of pork *(svinjski)* or veal *(teleći);* two skewers, the usual portion

Ćulbastija: grilled pork.

Order meat grilled over the coals *(na žaru)*, or go all the way and order one of the huge mixed grills *(miješano meso)*. Under the heading *Gotova jela* you'll find some tasty local specialities, mostly eaten at lunch time.

Djuveč: as if to prove that there's more to Yugoslavian cooking than kebabs, the Serbs invented this casserole dish of lamb or pork with rice, green pepper, eggplant, carrots, potatoes, cheese and whatever else captures the chef's imagination.

Sarma: an easy-to-pronounce, homey dish, this is cabbage leaves stuffed with minced meat and rice.

Musaka: layers of minced meat sauce alternating with potato, eggplant or courgettes (zucchini), baked.

Punjene paprike: green peppers stuffed with meat and rice in tomato sauce.

Pašticada: beef braised in wine served with noodles.

The more cautious diner can always order roast *(pečenje)*, specifying "hot" *(toplo)* or "cold" *(hladno)*.

What's your pleasure – Istra Bitter, *fiery* šljivovica *or just plain* pivo?

Fowl and Game
Piletina (chicken) and *ćuretina* (turkey) are commonly found on menus. But during hunting season you may want to try a more elusive bird such as *jarebica* (partridge) or *fazan* (pheasant).

Salads and Vegetables
Salads most frequently accompany the main dish in both simple and elegant restaurants. A favourite is *srpska salata* (Ser-

bian salad), a refreshing plate of tomatoes and onion. Another is *pečene paprike,* fried green pepper sprinkled with oil. Boiled vegetables also appear on the menus in season.

Cheese
Two authentic local cheeses are *Paški sir,* a hard, strong cheese from the island of Pag, and *Kačkavalj,* a medium-hard cheese of variable quality.

Good locally produced versions of popular European cheeses are widely available. For Yugoslavs, by the way, cheese is a starter rather than a final course, but no one will mind if you reverse the order.

Desserts
If you're not weight-watching, round off your meal with pancakes *(palačinke)* with ground nuts, jam or chocolate sauce. Sweet-lovers rave about the *baklava,* flaky pastry steeped in syrup, and other Turkish delights. Cream cakes and pastries of the Viennese type are often better in cake shops than in restaurants. The same applies to ice-cream.

Wines and Beer
Since the best Yugoslav wines are rarely found outside the country, you've some delightful surprises in store. Not least is the price—very reasonable

by Western standards, especially when bought in a shop or wine cellar.

Table wine *(stolno vino)* sold by the carafe is usually the local vintage, but none the worse for that. You can order as little as *tri deci* (three-tenths of a litre) to experiment. *Bjelo* (or *bijelo*) is white, *ružica* rosé, and *crno* (literally, black) means red wine. The locals often dilute it in the glass with soda or plain water.

Among the best-known Istrian wines are the reds, *Teran* (more powerful) and *Refoško* (lighter), and the whites, *Malvazija* (may be sweet or dry) and *Pinot*. The Kvarner Islands have a number of good wines as well.

Supermarkets in bigger resorts sell a bewildering variety of wines from all over Yugoslavia. Here are some of the outstanding ones from other regions:

Dingač: a full-bodied red from the Pelješac peninsula south of Split.

Grk: no vowels but plenty of punch in this strong white from the island of Korčula.

Kutjevo: varied wines of high standard from northern Croatia.

Prošek: a tawny-coloured dessert wine made along the coast from dried fermented grapes.

Vugava: a heady golden wine produced on the islands of Vis and Brač.

Žilavka: a delicate white wine from Herzegovina.

Slovenia produces some fine white wines *(Ljutomer Riesling, Jeruzalem, Ritoznojčan)*, not to mention the abundant output of Serbia and Macedonia.

If your thirst requires beer *(pivo)*, Yugoslavian lagers are sold in pint bottles. Imported brands, which are more expensive, come in smaller bottles.

Other Beverages

Bottled fruit juice *(voćni sok)* makes a refreshing drink—apricot, blueberry, peach, raspberry, strawberry, sour (morello) cherry, all trucked in from orchard country. Other soft drinks are also available, including several brand names, bottled locally. Prices for soft drinks, or any other kind of liquid refreshment, vary tremendously according to the ambiance, but they are posted in full view or listed on the

After-dinner activities may well include dancing under the stars.

Drop in and join the locals during their daily mid-morning break.

serve *cappuccino* and *eis kafe* (iced coffee with a scoop of ice-cream and whipped cream). Turkish coffee, served in tiny, long-handled pots, is a newcomer to these parts and not available everywhere. Its quality varies.

Liquor

Pre-dinner cocktails, a foreign invention, can be managed in many hotel bars. A Yugoslavian aperitif, milder than most, is *Istra Bitter,* a herb tonic. Imported brands of aperitifs, whiskies and other spirits are expensive.

Rakija is the generic term embracing all the brandies you're likely to find.

Šljivovica, plum brandy, is the most famous and popular Yugoslavian liquor.

Lozovača (grape brandy) and *kajsijevača* (apricot brandy) are alternative firewaters, according to your taste.

And don't forget *maraskino,* the liqueur made from maraschino, or morello, cherries.

Finally, *vinjak* is a local brandy reminiscent of a French cognac.

menu. Tea drinkers are likely to be disappointed.

Although the Yugoslavs are great coffee drinkers, at virtually any hour of the day or night, the coffee served in public places rarely compares favourably with what is drunk in the homes. Good espresso coffee is dispensed practically everywhere along the coast. If the normal half cup isn't enough, ask for a double portion *(dupli)*. Some cafés also

To Help You Order…

Could we have a table?	**Možemo li dobiti sto?**
The menu, please.	**Molim Vas, jelovnik.**
(I'd like some) … please.	**Molim Vas, …**
The bill, please.	**Molim Vas, račun.**

beer	**pivo**	napkin	**salvetu**
bread	**kruh**	potatoes	**krompir**
coffee	**kavu**	rice	**rižu**
cutlery	**pribor za jelo**	salad	**salatu**
dessert	**dezert**	sandwich	**sendvič**
fish	**ribu**	soup	**juhu**
fruit	**voće**	sugar	**šećer**
glass	**čašu**	tea	**čaj**
ice-cream	**sladoled**	water	**vodu**
meat	**meso**	wine	**vino**
milk	**mlijeko**	well-done	**dobro pečeno**
mineral water	**mineralnu vodu**	with ice	**sa ledom**

… and Read the Menu

ananas	pineapple	**fileki**	tripe
bakalar	codfish	**gljive**	mushrooms
barbun	red mullet	**govedina**	beef
biftek	beefsteak	**grašak**	peas
blitva	Swiss chard	**grožđe**	grapes
borovnice	blueberries	**gulaš**	goulash
brancin	sea-bass	**hladno**	cold
breskve	peaches	**hobotnica**	octopus
bubrežnjak	tenderloin	**hrenovka**	hot dog
cipal	grey mullet	**jabuka**	apple
češnjak	garlic	**jagnjetina**	lamb
čokolada	chocolate	**jagode**	strawberries
čorba	thick soup	**jaja**	eggs
dagnje	mussels	**jastog**	lobster
dinja	melon	**jetra**	liver
divljač	game	**junetina**	baby beef
fažol	dried beans	**kalamari**	squid
file	fillet	**kamenice**	oysters

93

kavijar	caviar
keks	biscuits (cookies)
kiselo mlijeko	yoghurt
kobasice	sausages
kompot	stewed fruit
kotlet	chop
kovač	John Dory (fish)
krastavac	cucumber
krem	cream pudding
krompir	potatoes
kruška	pear
kuhano	boiled
kupus	cabbage
lešo	boiled
lignje	squid
limun	lemon
list	sole
lubenica	watermelon
luk	onion
mahune	string beans
maline	raspberries
marelice	apricots
maslac	butter
masline	olives
meso	meat
miješano	mixed
mladica	trout
mrkva	carrots
mušule	mussels
na gradele / na roštilju / na žaru	grilled
na ražanj	barbecued on a spit
nar	pomegranate
narandža	orange
odojak	sucking pig
odrezak	cutlet
orada	bream
oslić	hake
ovčetina	mutton
paprika	green pepper
pečenje	roast
piletina	chicken
pljeskavica	hamburger steak
polpete	meatballs
povrće	vegetables
prepržen kruh	toast
prstaci	mussels
pršut	smoked ham
prženo	fried
račići	shrimp
ragu	stew
rajčica	tomato
rak	crab
riba	fish
riža	rice
salama	salami
salata	salad
sardela	anchovy
sendvič	sandwich
sir	cheese
skampi	prawns
skuša	mackerel
sladoled	ice-cream
smokve	figs
svinjetina	pork
školjke	shellfish
špinat	spinach
šunka	ham
teletina	veal
toplo	hot
torta	cake
trešnje	cherries
tunina	tunny (tuna)
umak	sauce
vešalica	grilled veal or pork
višnje	sour cherries
vrhnje	whipped cream
zelena salata	lettuce salad
zubatac	dentex (fish)

How to Get There

Fares and routes for local and international transport—whether by rail, sea, air, road or a combination of these—are constantly changing. Your travel agent should have the most up-to-date information.

From Great Britain

BY AIR. Scheduled, direct flights operate regularly to the Istrian airport of Pula from London. Travellers leaving from most British provincial airports, as well as Dublin, can make same-day connections to Pula or Rijeka via London, Amsterdam or Zurich and Zagreb or Belgrade. Trieste airport is also convenient for the west-coast Istrian resorts.

Charter Flights and Package Tours. The all-inclusive package tour —combining flight, hotel and board—remains a most popular way of visiting the Yugoslavian Adriatic coast. Most travel agents recommend cancellation insurance, a modestly priced safeguard: you lose no money if illness or accident forces you to cancel your holiday.

BY CAR. In July and August, with cross-Channel car-ferry and hovercraft space at a premium, be sure to book well in advance.

Whether you prefer the shorter northern route through Belgium, Germany and Austria and the southern one through France and Italy, you'll be able to drive on motorways (expressways) almost all the way (paying tolls in France and Italy).

If you don't fancy the three- to five-day haul across Europe, put your car on a train (Brussels–Ljubljana or Paris–Munich–Rijeka). Both services operate only during the summer season, however. The car-sleeper motor-rail express, while expensive, saves on fuel, wear and tear and hotel bills. You can take to the wheel again in Ljubljana or Rijeka and sightsee refreshed.

BY RAIL. From London, there are two main express trains to the Istria region: Ostend–Ljubljana and the Simplon Express (via Paris to Trieste or Divača, on the line for Pula).

Inter-Rail Card. This ticket permits 30 days of unlimited rail travel in participating European countries (and Morocco) to people under 26. In the country of issue, fares are given a 50 per cent discount. Senior citizens can purchase the **Rail Europe Senior Card** for unlimited travel, allowing a discount of 30 to 50%.

From North America

BY AIR. There is regular direct service to Belgrade from Chicago and New York. Daily connecting flights may be booked from another two dozen American cities, as well as from Calgary, Montreal, Toronto and Vancouver. More than 40 cities in the U.S. have flights to Belgrade on specific days of the week (usually not Mondays and Thursdays). Vienna is the most popular gateway city.

Although direct service to Zagreb from New York and Chicago is less frequent, there are daily connecting flights from various American cities, as well as from Montreal and Toronto.

Charter Flights and Package Tours. Tours of Yugoslavia vary from three to 11 nights. The all-inclusive price covers hotel accommodation, airport transfers, all or most meals, sightseeing, English-speaking guide, plus hotel taxes and service charges. Yugoslavia can also be visited on tours of Eastern Europe and Russia.

When to Go

The northern Adriatic enjoys hot summers and mild winters, with resorts like Opatija and sheltered towns on the west coast of Istria attracting tourists all year round. In summer, gentle breezes bring a welcome freshness, and the sea here is just as warm as it is further down the coast. Chilly and rainy spells are rarities. At other times of the year, strong northern winds like the *bura* prevail in some exposed areas.

To avoid the crowds, try June and September; the weather is only slightly cooler than in July and August.

Air temperature		J	F	M	A	M	J	J	A	S	O	N	D
Poreč:	°F	47	47	52	59	66	73	77	79	73	64	55	50
	°C	8	8	11	15	19	23	25	26	23	18	13	10
Opatija:	°F	47	48	53	62	68	77	82	82	75	64	55	51
	°C	8	9	12	17	20	25	28	28	24	18	13	11

Sea temperature		J	F	M	A	M	J	J	A	S	O	N	D
Poreč:	°F	52	48	50	55	63	70	73	75	73	66	61	55
	°C	11	9	10	13	17	21	23	24	23	19	16	13
Opatija:	°F	46	45	46	52	60	68	74	73	70	62	56	51
	°C	8	7	8	11	15	20	23	23	21	17	13	10

Figures shown are approximate monthly averages.

BLUEPRINT for a Perfect Trip

An A-Z Summary of Practical Information and Facts

> Listed after each main entry is its appropriate Serbo-Croatian translation, usually in the singular. You'll find this vocabulary useful when asking for assistance. Because of the linguistic variations you may encounter in different regions, an alternative translation is sometimes indicated in brackets [ ]. If the first expression brings a blank look, try the second.

A ACCOMMODATION—see **HOTELS**

AIRPORT *(aerodrom)*. The principal airports serving Istria are Rijeka and Pula. Trieste and Ljubljana are also within easy reach.

There is an airport tax both for domestic and international flights.

Rijeka Airport on the northern tip of the island of Krk is linked with Zagreb, Belgrade, Split and Dubrovnik by JAT (Yugoslav Airlines). Transport to Rijeka and Črišnjeva from the airport is guaranteed by bus or ferry. Charter flights are met by tourist-agency buses. Transport to other destinations (by taxi, hired car and even air taxi) and hotel accommodation can be arranged at the airport. There's a duty-free shop, a snack bar, and a currency-exchange counter. Check-in time at the terminal: 60 minutes before take-off for domestic flights, 70 minutes for international flights.

Pula Airport is mainly used for charters and seasonal lines (services to Belgrade and Zagreb). JAT buses take passengers to the centre of Pula (main bus station) in about 15 minutes. The airport has car-rental and travel agencies, a restaurant and a duty-free shop. Check-in time at the terminal is 30 minutes for domestic flights, 60 minutes for international.

Porter!	**Nosač!**
Where's the bus for...?	**Gde je autobus za...?**

ALPHABET. Two alphabets are used in Yugoslavia: the familiar Latin and the Cyrillic, similar to Greek or Russian, used mainly in Serbia, Montenegro and Macedonia. You're unlikely to see Cyrillic except on news-stands. Both alphabets are completely phonetic, so it's easy to read Serbo-Croatian once you know how each letter is pronounced. The Latin letters not given below are pronounced much the same as in English.

A	c*ar*	**C**	ba*ts*	**J**	*y*oke
E	g*e*t	**Č**	*ch*urch	**LJ**	fai*lu*re
I	l*ea*p	**Ć**	crun*chier*	**NJ**	o*ni*on
O	p*o*t	**DŽ**	*j*eep	**Š**	*sh*ip
U	b*oo*m	**DJ**	sol*di*er	**Ž**	plea*s*ure

BABYSITTERS *(čuvanje dece)*. Babysitting facilities aren't likely to be available on an organized basis—except in luxury hotels. In out-of-the-way spots, somebody's grandmother will probably be recruited. Ask your hotel desk-clerk or at the travel-agency office in your resort.

Can you get us a babysitter for tonight?	**Možete li nam naći nekog da čuva decu večeras?**

BANKS and CURRENCY-EXCHANGE OFFICES *(banka; menjačnica)*. Banks open early in summer—7 a.m. in many resorts—and close anywhere from 11.30 a.m. to 7 p.m.

When banks are closed or too far away, you can change money at identical rates in authorized currency-exchange offices including travel agencies and hotels. Though currency-exchange operations may close a few hours for lunch, they usually remain open until early evening.

Try to assess how much dinar cash you will need, because excess cash cannot be reconverted, and only a small amount can be exported (see CUSTOMS CONTROLS).

I want to change some pounds/ dollars.	**Želim da promenim funte/ dolare.**

BARBER'S—see **HAIRDRESSER'S**

BICYCLES *(bicikl)*. Bicycles can be hired by the hour in a few resorts, but it's not possible to hire one—or any other two-wheeled vehicle—for longer excursions.

B **BOAT SERVICES** *(brodske veze)*. Passenger steamers, car ferries and fast hydrofoils operate up and down the coast and between the mainland and the islands. At the peak of the summer, certain lines are crowded, particularly the car ferries, so you may prefer to leave your car on the mainland. Tickets may be purchased at the local booking office *(Jadrolinija)*, at the dock or even on board. Book cabins in advance for overnight trips. Refreshments are usually available on board.

Car ferry *(trajekt)*. Fares depend on the size of the car and the number of passengers. The driver travels free. With a caravan (trailer) the fares are twice as high. It's cheaper to go to the ferry crossing nearest to your destination.

I'd like a ticket to ...   **Želeo bih kartu za ...**

BOY MEETS GIRL. Attitudes towards life are relaxed along the Adriatic. The flirtation is comparable to anywhere else in Europe. As in most countries, however, beware that small towns are much more strict than cities and tourist-trampled zones. If you haven't made friends on the beach, take in the *korzo*—the community promenade—at sunset. In every town, the main square or street is a meeting point for all the young people who stroll and chat and look the field over to plan the evening's activities.

BUS SERVICES *(autobusni transport)*. Regional bus transport is highly developed, usually comfortable and not expensive. Most towns have a bus station where seats can be booked ahead when buying a ticket. Posted timetables are complicated: it's safer to inquire about times at your hotel or local tourist office. Sometimes an excursion is cheaper by regular bus than by an organized tour (see EXCURSIONS).

   City transport is cheap but crowded at rush hours and at the height of the summer season. Queues are a relatively new practice not often observed at bus stops. You get on city buses at the rear and pay the conductor seated next to the door. Exit by the middle or front door.

When's the next bus to...?   **Kad ide sledeći autobus za...?**

single (one way)   **u jednom pravcu**
100 return (roundtrip)   **povratnu kartu**

CAMPING *(kampovanje)*. Istria, the Croatian Littoral and the Kvarner islands have over 60 campsites, many in pine woods near the shoreline. Camping isn't allowed outside organized sites. Rates vary according to category and location. Holders of an international camping *carnet* (card) get a discount. Half a dozen naturist campsites are located in Yugoslavia, most of them in Istria.

The Automobile Association of Yugoslavia (AMSJ) publishes annually a list of campsites—indicating facilities offered and fees—in English, French, German and Italian. These lists are available at Yugoslav National Tourist offices, at AMSJ and at local tourist offices in Yugoslavia.

Is there a campsite near here?	**Da li ima kamp u blizini?**
May we camp here?	**Možemo li ovde kampovati?**
What's the charge ...?	**Koliko košta ...?**
per person	**po osobi**
for a car	**za kola**
for a tent	**za šator**
for a caravan (trailer)	**za prikolicu**

CAR RENTAL *(rent a kar)*. Half a dozen car-rental firms have agencies in Istria and northern Yugoslavia and at its airports. If you haven't reserved a car before leaving home, your hotel desk-clerk can put you in touch with the nearest agency.

Rates vary with the firm, the model of car, the length of time you use it and whether you plan to return it to the same place or elsewhere in Yugoslavia or abroad. The most frequently rented cars are Volkswagens, Renaults, Fiats and Audis. A Mercedes 220 will cost twice the price of a VW. Chauffeured cars can also be hired.

You must pay a refundable deposit unless you hold an internationally recognized credit card. A local tax may or may not be included in the rate. Non-deductible collision insurance and accident insurance, covering driver and passengers, come extra. Fuel and traffic fines are the customer's responsibility.

You must, of course, have a valid driving licence at least two years old. The minimum age is generally 21.

I'd like to rent a car tomorrow.	**Hteo bih da rentiram kola.**
for one day/a week	**za jedan dan/jednu nedelju**
Please include full insurance.	**Sa potpunim osiguranjem molim Vas.**

101

C

CHURCH SERVICES. Mass is said daily in many towns of this predominantly Roman Catholic region. Hotels or agencies sometimes organize services for Protestant church-goers.

What time is mass/the service?	**U koliko sati je misa/služba?**
Is it in English?	**Da li je na engleskom jeziku?**

CIGARETTES, CIGARS, TOBACCO *(cigarete, cigare, duvan)*. Yugoslavian cigarettes come in a strong, black Turkish variety as well as in mild blends similar to western European cigarettes. In addition to many local makes, certain American brands are manufactured in Yugoslavia under licence. In larger towns and resorts a few British brands may also be found. As in most countries, the local cigarettes cost only a fraction of the retail price of the imports.

Tobacco shops also sell imported (usually Cuban) cigars and Yugoslavian pipe tobacco, which is highly regarded by connoisseurs.

A packet of cigarettes/matches.	**Kutiju cigareta/šibica.**
filter-tipped	**sa filterom**
without filter	**bez filtera**
light tobacco	**blagi duvan**
dark tobacco	**ljuti duvan**

CLOTHING *(odevanje)*. With its Mediterranean climate, the Istrian coast demands lightweight clothing from June to September—the lighter the better. But on the fringes of the high season—before July and after September—you may well need a jacket or sweater for the evening. Although the rainy season comes in winter, you could need a raincoat at any time of year.

Formality in dress is confined to sophisticated night-clubs and casinos. Elsewhere it's a matter of pleasing yourself. That goes for beaches as well; no prudish anti-bikini sentiments here. However, it's reasonable to slip something over your bathing suit for the walk to and from the beach.

Obviously, when visiting churches modest dress is appropriate. And don't forget to wear your comfortable shoes when you go visiting museums or sightseeing.

When buying shoes or clothing, the following conversion table should be useful (remember though that sizes vary somewhat according to manufacturers):

Women								
Clothing			Shirts / Pullovers			Shoes		
GB	USA	YU	GB	USA	YU	GB	USA	YU
10	8	40	32	10	38	3	4½	35
12	10	42	34	12	40	4	5½	36
14	12	44	36	14	42	5	6½	37
16	14	46	38	16	44	6	7½	38

Men						
Clothing		Shirts		Shoes		
GB / USA	YU	GB / USA	YU	GB	USA	YU
36	46	14	36	6	6½	40
38	48	14½	37	7	7½	41
40	50	15	38	8	8½	42
42	52	15½	39	9	9½	43
44	54	16	40	10	10½	44

COMPLAINTS *(žalba)*. Complaint procedures are far less formalized in Yugoslavia than they've become in some other countries.

Hotels and restaurants. See the manager if you're dissatisfied. If this leads nowhere, the local tourist office may suggest further steps.

Bad merchandise. The consumer-oriented society is too new in Yugoslavia to have devised elaborate safeguards. Your best bet here is to return to the shop which sold you the article and appeal to the manager's sense of fair play. If you've got a serious gripe, the *tržišna inspekcija* (market-control board) in large towns can be of help in sorting things out.

Car repairs. If your car has been badly repaired, or if you believe you've been overcharged, try to settle the problem before paying the bill. If this fails, a local travel office or the *tržišna inspekcija* (market-control board) may be able to mediate or advise.

Other services. By law, prices should be posted, but to avoid misunderstanding, it's wise to ask the cost of all services in advance.

C   **CONSULATES** *(konzulat)*

British Consulate*: Ilica 12, Zagreb; tel. (041) 424-888.

U.S. Consulate: Braće Kavurića 2, 41000 Zagreb; tel. (041) 444-800.

Where's the British/American Consulate?	**Gde je Britanski/Američki konzulat?**

CONVERSION TABLES. For fluid measures and tire pressure—see page 108. Yugoslavia uses the metric system.

Length

1 centimetre = 0.39 in. (approx. 2/5 in.)	1 in. = 2.54 cm
1 metre = 39.40 in. (approx. 3 ft., 3 in.)	1 yd. = 91.44 cm
1 kilometre = 0.621 mile (approx. 6/10 mile)	1 mile = 1.61 km

Weight

200 grams = 0.441 lb. (approx. 7 oz.)	¼ lb. = 113.40 g
1 kilogram = 2.205 lbs. (approx. 2 lbs., 3 oz.)	1 lb. = 453.60 g

Temperature

To convert centigrade into Fahrenheit, multiply by 1.8 and add 32. To convert Fahrenheit into centigrade, subtract 32 and divide by 1.8.

COURTESIES. See also BOY MEETS GIRL. Most of the precepts for getting along with people anywhere apply to Yugoslavia—be friendly, be yourself, be reasonable. If the locals put ice-cubes in their drinks and you don't, or vice versa, don't let it keep you awake at night.

Speaking of drinks, if a Yugoslav offers you one, it's just about obligatory to accept. If you're not in the mood for brandy, say yes to coffee. You aren't expected to stand the next round; the hospitality can be returned at a later date. If you're a house guest or otherwise treated to a great deal of food, drink and kindness, you may reciprocate by buying a small gift, preferably for any children in the family. Children are very important in the Yugoslavian scheme of things. (Notice the young couples proudly promenading with their offspring.)

All this old-fashioned central European courtesy (though we're in the Balkans, traces of the centuries of Austrian influence remain) is suddenly forgotten in less relaxed situations—such as clambering aboard a crowded bus. *Izvinite* (excuse me) is about all one can say.

Always ask permission before taking photos of people.

* also for citizens of Commonwealth countries

CREDIT CARDS and TRAVELLERS' CHEQUES *(kreditna karta; putni ček)*

Credit cards: Diner's Club and American Express are the most widely accepted cards. Although many hotels, restaurants and tourist-oriented enterprises accept credit cards, they're by no means known everywhere, particularly in the villages.

Travellers' cheques: These may be changed at banks, hotels and travel agencies and are accepted in many shops and restaurants. You'll almost certainly be asked to show your passport when cashing a cheque.

Dinar cheques. You will have to check when changing money if they still exist (the question seems to hover in a permanently unsettled state), but dinar cheques can help you make savings. Foreigners can use these cheques for most kinds of goods and services within the country (any difference between the value of the cheque and the service rendered is made up in change).

Do you accept travellers' cheques?	**Da li primate putne čekove?**
Can I pay with this credit card?	**Mogu li da platim kreditnom kartom?**

CRIME and THEFTS *(zločin; kradja).* In the event of a crime, you may indeed have trouble finding a policeman to assist you. But the nearest travel office or hotel desk should be able to put you in quick touch with the *milicija* (police).

Crime persists under all known social systems, so don't tempt fate by leaving your valuables imprudently unprotected or exposed.

I want to report a theft.	**Želim da prijavim kradju.**

CURRENCY *(valuta).* The monetary unit of Yugoslavia is the *dinar* (abbreviated *din.*). Sometimes the dinar is referred to as *novi dinar* (new dinar). In conversation, Yugoslavs may refer to *stari dinar* (old dinar), 100 of which make a new dinar.

Coins: 1, 2, 5, 10, 20, 50, 100 dinars.
Banknotes: 10, 20, 50, 100, 500, 1,000, 2,000, 5,000 dinars.

CUSTOMS CONTROLS. See also ENTRY FORMALITIES. The best policy with customs men anywhere is to tell the truth if they ask any questions; being caught after replying "inexactly" could be embarrassing.

C Here's what you can bring into Yugoslavia duty-free:

Cigarettes	Cigars	Tobacco	Spirits	Wine
200 or	50 or	250 g.	1 l. and	1 l.

While you may bring unlimited sums of foreign currency into Yugoslavia, you may not carry more than 5,000 dinars (in denominations
no larger than 1,000 dinars) across the border in either direction, and
this amount can only be imported or exported once per calendar year.
On subsequent trips, a maximum of 2,000 dinars may be imported or
exported.

Souvenirs and duty-free wine and tobacco products are sold at
Yugoslavian airports.

I've nothing to declare.	**Nemam ništa za carinjenje.**
It's for personal use.	**To je za moju ličnu upotrebu.**

D **DRIVING IN YUGOSLAVIA**

Entering Yugoslavia: To bring your car into Yugoslavia you'll need:

● A valid driving licence; an International Driving Licence is recom-
mended but not required
● Car registration papers
● Green Card (international insurance certificate)

The nationality code sticker must be visible at the rear of the car.
You must possess a red-reflector warning triangle for use in case of
breakdown, a first-aid kit and a spare set of headlight bulbs. Seat belts
are compulsory.

All resorts and most other places of interest are linked by asphalt
roads. Secondary roads tend to be fairly narrow and winding.

There are no toll roads except on two short stretches of motorway
(expressway) between Zagreb and Karlovac and from Ljubljana towards Koper.

Be certain you have a clear view ahead before attempting to over-
take. Unforeseen obstructions, such as pedestrians, donkeys or ox
carts, may catch you off guard.

Quaint local attractions may become deadly perils on the road.
When passing through villages, drive with extra care to avoid children

darting out of doorways and older folk strolling in the middle of the
road, particularly after dark. You'll need steely self-control to resist
looking around at the spectacular scenery. Better to stop more often to
really enjoy the views.

Another word of warning: Yugoslavia has stringent regulations
about drinking and driving—allowing only 0.5 per mil alcohol content
in the blood instead of 0.8 as in Great Britain and most of Western
Europe. Violations can lead to stiff fines or 60 days in jail.

Speed limits: Unless otherwise indicated, 60 kilometres per hour in
towns, 80 or 100 kph outside of towns (120 kph on motorways). A car
with a caravan (trailer) mustn't exceed 80 kilometres per hour, even on
the open road.

Traffic police *(saobraćajna milicija)* : In summer, in major towns and
resorts, the traffic police are easily seen with their white helmets and
white uniforms. Some cities employ white-uniformed students to help
direct traffic and give information. They usually speak at least one
foreign language. Off-season, the traffic police wear grey-blue uniforms. Police cars are blue and white with a roof light and are often
parked at busy road junctions. Reckless or drunken driving may be
treated very severely. For other infractions—such as ignoring a stop
sign or breaking speed limits—the driver may be fined on the spot.
(The defendant is entitled to demand a court hearing, but this is a
time-consuming way to prove a principle.)

Fuel and oil: Not every crossroads boasts a filling station but the coast
is reasonably well supplied with them. Two grades of petrol are sold:
premium (86 octane) and super (98 octane). Diesel fuel is normally
also available.

Well-known brands of motor oils may be bought at garages and
shops.

Petrol coupons: These coupons can be bought at travel agencies, at
automobile clubs in the country of departure, at the Yugoslav frontier
or from an authorized exchange dealer in Yugoslavia, and mean a
slight reduction in the petrol prices. Unused coupons are refunded at
the border when leaving the country or at the place where they were
bought. NB: ask your automobile association about the latest regulations, as they are constantly changing.

Note that it is prohibited to enter Yugoslavia with a spare can of
petrol in the car.

D Fluid measures

imp. gals. 0 ──────────── 5 ──────────── 10

litres 0 — 5 — 10 ──── 20 ──── 30 ──── 40 ──── 50

U.S. gals. 0 ──────────── 5 ──────────── 10

Tire pressure			
lb./sq. in.	kg/cm²	lb./sq. in.	kg/cm²
10	0.7	26	1.8
12	0.8	27	1.9
15	1.1	28	2.0
18	1.3	30	2.1
20	1.4	33	2.3
21	1.5	36	2.5
23	1.6	38	2.7
24	1.7	40	2.8

Breakdowns: The Automobile Association of Yugoslavia (Auto-Moto Savez Jugoslavije, AMSJ) runs aid and information offices in major towns. They're open from 8 a.m. to 8 p.m. You can call on them for help in many towns, usually by dialling 987; rates charged for road and tow services are cheaper than those of garages.

Garages specializing in the repair of the leading makes of cars are found only in the larger cities. Privately run garages elsewhere can probably tide you over with ingenious stop-gap methods. But insist on a realistic price estimate in advance. If you need replacement parts there may be a problem of long delays. Spare parts are readily available for cars assembled in Yugoslavia: Citroën, Fiat, Renault, Volkswagen and the Zastava 101. The automobile association can help with urgent shipments. Naturally, an ounce of prevention—a thorough check of your car before you ever leave home—can avoid many a holiday headache on the road.

Parking: Parking conditions vary. Some towns have a lot of free parking space, others charge a few dinars in central locations, near the beach or at some other attraction. In larger towns there are parking meters or blue zones. Incidentally, wherever you park—in town or on a country road—the law requires you do so on the right-hand side, never facing the flow of traffic. If you leave your car in a no-parking zone it may be towed away.

Road signs: The standard international picture-signs are in general use throughout Yugoslavia. But here are a few of the more common written notices you may encounter:

Aerodrom	Airport
Automehaničar	Car mechanic
Centar grada	Town centre
Garaža	Garage
Milicija	Police
Odron kamena	Falling rocks
Opasna krivina	Dangerous curve
Opasnost	Danger
Radovi na putu	Road works (Men working)
Stoj	Stop
Škola	School
Uspon	Steep hill

(International) Driving Licence	**(medjunarodna) vozačka dozvola**
Car registration papers	**saobraćajna dozvola**
Green Card	**zelena karta**

Are we on the right road for …?	**Da li je ovo put za…?**
Full tank please, top grade.	**Napunite molim Vas, super.**
Check the oil/tires/battery.	**Proverite ulje/gume/akumulator.**
I've had a breakdown.	**Kola su mi u kvaru.**
There's been an accident.	**Dogodio se nesrećni slučaj.**

DRUGS. The authorities take a very dim view of anyone choosing Yugoslavia as a corridor for drug smuggling.

ELECTRIC CURRENT *(električna struja).* The standard voltage in Yugoslavia is 220-volt, 50-cycle A.C. American appliances will need transformers and plug adapters.

If your hair-dryer or other electric appliance breaks down, ask your hotel desk-clerk if he can recommend an electrical repair shop or local handyman to rescue you.

I'd like an adapter/	**Želim adaptor/**
a battery.	**bateriju.**

109

EMBASSIES—see **CONSULATES**

EMERGENCIES. Depending on the nature of the emergency, refer to the separate entries in this section such as CONSULATES, MEDICAL CARE, POLICE, etc. If there's no time, put your problem into the hands of your hotel desk-clerk, travel agency or a taxi driver.

Though we hope you'll never need them, here are a few key words you might like to learn as insurance:

Careful	**Oprezno**	Police	**Milicija**
Fire	**Vatra**	Stop	**Stanite**
Help	**U pomoć**	Stop thief	**Držite lopova**

ENTRY FORMALITIES. See also CUSTOMS CONTROLS. All travellers must carry valid passports. Citizens of Great Britain and Ireland may enter Yugoslavia without visas or formalities. American, Australian and Canadian citizens are automatically given entry visas upon arrival. Of course, if in doubt about visa formalities, it's wise to check with your travel agent before you leave home. You're generally entitled to stay in Yugoslavia for up to 90 days.

Residents of the British Isles, continental Europe and North America need no health certificate to enter Yugoslavia. If you're coming from further afield, you may need an international smallpox certificate, so check beforehand.

EXCURSIONS *(izlet)*. Every tourist office and hotel has day and half-day trips by bus or boat prominently advertised. Prices are invariably uniform: no need to shop around. If you feel like going alone, compare normal bus or steamer fares (see BUS SERVICES, BOAT SERVICES). It may be as convenient, and is certainly considerably cheaper, to use public transportation. This applies to shorter excursions and not to full-day organized trips visiting several places: a time-consuming and complicated chore to undertake unless you have your own car. Check if the tour price includes a meal, and, if not, order a picnic lunch the night before from your hotel desk-clerk. Otherwise inquire about refreshments available en route.

It's wiser not to plan any sidetrips on the first and last days of July and August when everyone is going on holiday or returning bumper to
bumper.

FIRE. Forest fires are a real menace in summer so be very careful where you throw your cigarette butts and matches. Note that some zones—clearly marked—prohibit both smoking and open fires. If you're enjoying a legal campfire, don't forget to extinguish it and douse it with water before leaving.

F

GUIDES and INTERPRETERS *(vodič; tumač)*. The average tourist won't need any special assistance. Hotel personnel can deal with most linguistic problems, and the travel agencies provide competent multilingual guides to conduct their tours.

G

However, if you need personalized interpreting or guidance for business or pleasure, apply to one of the travel agencies in the nearest city or resort.

We'd like an English-speaking guide.	**Hteli bismo engleskog vodiča.**
I need an English interpreter.	**Trebam tumača za engleski jezik.**

HAGGLING *(cenkanje)*. Almost without exception shops in Yugoslavia post their prices and stick by them; haggling might be considered offensive. But if you're shopping for souvenirs at outdoor bazaars or from pushcart-pedlars, by all means try to negotiate a better price.

H

HAIRDRESSER'S and BEAUTY SALONS *(frizer; kozmetički salon)*. Prices are more than double if you patronize the salons in luxury hotels rather than neighbourhood shops.

Tip about 10 per cent.

haircut	**šišanje**
shampoo and set	**pranje kose i češljanje**
permanent wave	**trajna ondulacija**
manicure	**manikir**
shave	**brijanje**
a colour chart	**pregled boja**
a colour rinse	**preliv**
Not too much off (here).	**Nemojte suviše odrezati (ovde).**
A little more off (here).	**Odrežite još malo (ovde).**
How much do I owe you?	**Koliko sam dužan?**

111

H **HEALTH.** Most tourists who suffer health problems in Yugoslavia have only themselves to blame—for overdoing the sunshine and inexpensive alcohol. If you want to protect a delicate stomach, take it easy on the adventurous foods for the first few days and stick to the excellent mineral waters. See also MEDICAL CARE.

HITCH-HIKING *(autostop)*. It's permitted but it isn't always care-free. A high percentage of passing cars are loaded with passengers and luggage.

Can you give me a lift to ...?　　　**Možete li me povesti do ...?**

HOTELS and ACCOMMODATION *(hotel; smeštaj)*. Hotels in Yugoslavia are officially graded in five categories. L is deluxe, and from there the classifications descend from A to D, the latter being the lowest grade which earns the title hotel. The classifications are designed to give you an idea of what facilities are offered and what they should cost.

Luxury hotels, extremely rare, measure up to the highest international standards. Full board in a luxury hotel may cost twice as much as the room rate in a slightly less elegant A-class hotel. Breakfast is usually included in the room rate in higher-category hotels. Full-board rates are more economical, but a three-day stay is the minimum.

Most travel agents can supply a hotel list showing rates and facilities. Prices are considerably reduced during off-season. Also, for long stays you can normally get a reduction on the daily rate. A tourist tax is charged to every traveller whether he stays in a hotel or is camping. The amount depends on the season and local regulations.

Other forms of accommodation:

A **pansion** (boarding house) sometimes has fewer facilities than a hotel. They're graded in three categories: I to III. Prices run about the same as C-category hotels.

A **turističko naselje** ("tourist village") may consist of bungalows or pavilions sprawling around a central core of restaurants and public lounges.

A **motel** (motel), a recent innovation along Yugoslav highways, is sometimes tied in with car-repair facilities.

A **stan** or **vila** (apartment/villa) is a popular type of holiday accommodation for many visitors to Yugoslavia but may be difficult to arrange at the last moment. Write to the tourist office of the resort of your choice.

Soba (room); in popular resorts rooms in private homes often outnumber hotel rooms. They're closely supervised and graded (from I to IV), according to the degree of comfort provided and location. Accommodation can be arranged through the local tourist office. Landladies canvassing near ferry and bus terminals offer rooms to arriving tourists.

Whether all your problems have been solved far in advance by a package-tour operator, or you arrive without any warning, housing can certainly be arranged. However, at the height of the season the unexpected visitor may have to settle for an extremely modest roof over his head. Out of season, there's usually a 20 per cent reduction in rates.

a double/single room	**soba sa dva kreveta/sa jednim krevetom**
with/without bath	**sa kupatilom/bez kupatila**
What's the rate per night?	**Koliko staje za jednu noć?**

HOURS (see also BANKS and POST OFFICES)

Consulates are usually open from 8 or 8.30 a.m. to 12.30 or 1 p.m. and reopen between 1.30–3.30 to 5 p.m., Monday to Friday (some close in the afternoon on certain weekdays).

Offices: 7 a.m. to 2 or 3 p.m., Monday to Friday.

Shops: 8 a.m. to noon and 5 to 8 p.m., Monday to Friday, 8 a.m. to 2 or 3 on Saturdays. Most self-service shops, department stores and food shops, however, are open non-stop.

INTERPRETERS—see **GUIDES**

LANGUAGE. Few countries can claim a more confusing linguistic situation. In Yugoslavia, there are three major languages with equal status and two alphabets (see ALPHABET). Along the coast the language is the Croatian variant of Serbo-Croatian. Yugoslavia's other two

L languages are Slovenian (spoken in the north-west) and Macedonian (spoken in the south-east). The three closely resemble one another so a smattering of Serbo-Croatian will serve you in any part of Yugoslavia.

Italian is widely spoken along the coast. Other languages—Albanian, Bulgarian, Hungarian, Romanian, Slovakian, Turkish—are used by minorities in different regions of the nation, and English and German are widely understood along the coast.

A few words in Serbo-Croatian or Slovenian, though, will go far in producing a smile of friendship.

	Serbo-Croatian	Slovenian
Good morning	*Dobro jutro*	*Dobro jutro*
Good afternoon	*Dobar dan*	*Dober dan*
Good evening	*Dobro veče*	*Dober večer*
Thank you	*Hvala*	*Hvala*
You're welcome	*Nema na čemu*	*Ni za kaj*
Please	*Molim*	*Prosim*
Goodbye	*Zbogom*	*Na svidenje*

The Berlitz phrase book SERBO-CROATIAN FOR TRAVELLERS covers almost all situations you're likely to encounter in your travels in Yugoslavia.

Does anybody here speak English? **Da li neko ovde govori engleski?**

LAUNDRY and DRY-CLEANING *(pranje rublja; hemijsko čišćenje)*. Most hotels will handle your laundry and dry-cleaning relatively swiftly. Otherwise, you can go to a local laundry or dry-cleaner's, which in any case will be cheaper. Coin-operated launderettes don't exist yet along the coast.

When will it be ready? **Kada će biti gotovo?**
I must have this for tomorrow morning. **Ovo mi treba za sutra ujutro.**

LAWYERS and LEGAL SERVICES *(advokat; pravna usluga)*. In case of serious trouble, ask your consulate for advice.

If your problem stems from a road mishap and you're a member of a motoring or touring association at home, free legal advice may be obtained from the Automobile Association of Yugoslavia.

LOST AND FOUND PROPERTY; LOST CHILDREN (*biro za na-djene stvari; izgubljeno dete*). Inquire first at your hotel desk or the nearest tourist office. Then report the loss to the *milicija* (police).

As for lost children, hotel personnel are accustomed to these crises and will help with sympathy and knowledgeable action.

I've lost my wallet.	**Izgubio sam novčanik [lisnicu].**
I've lost my handbag.	**Izgubila sam tašnu.**

MAIL (*pošta*). If you're uncertain of your holiday address, you may have letters sent to you, care of poste restante (general delivery) at the local post office. Mail should be addressed as follows:

> Mr. John Smith
> Post Restant
> Poreč
> Yugoslavia

In large cities where there's more than one post office, mail may be picked up at the town's main post office.

When you claim your mail you'll have to produce your passport as identification.

Have you any mail for me?   **Ima li pošte za mene?**

MAPS (*karta*). Yugoslav National Tourist Offices in your country issue free maps pinpointing resort areas.

On the spot, bookshops along the coast sell maps with greater detail. For the most serious explorers, the Yugoslav Lexicographical Institute has produced *The Yugoslav Coast, Guide Book and Atlas.* This impressively researched book contains listings for hundreds of towns and villages, plus 27 maps.

a street plan of...	**plan grada...**
a road map of this region	**cestovna karta ovog kraja**

MEDICAL CARE (*lekarska usluga*). See also EMERGENCIES. Citizens of half a dozen western European countries—including Great Britain—are entitled to free medical care under reciprocal agreements with Yugoslavia. Citizens of other countries must pay for medical services.

M

For help in minor emergencies look for an *apoteka* or *ljekarna* (chemist's or drugstore) or an *ambulanta* (first-aid post) displaying a red cross.

Pharmacies. In an *apoteka* you'll find both non-prescription medicines and those made up according to a prescription. In a *drogerija* you'll find a great range of toilet articles, cosmetics and the like, sometimes films, too.

In the window of an *apoteka* you'll see a notice telling you where the nearest all-night chemist is. In larger towns, some chemists are open day and night. Their names and addresses can be found in daily newspapers.

If you're required to take certain medicine regularly, it would be wise to stock up before you leave home. Specific brands of medicine might not always be available locally in Yugoslavia.

Where's the nearest pharmacy?	**Gde je najbliža apoteka?**
a dentist	**zubni lekar**
a doctor	**lekar [doktor]**
an ambulance	**kola za hitnu pomoć**
hospital	**bolnica**
an upset stomach	**pokvaren stomak**
sunstroke	**sunčanica**
a fever	**groznica**

MOPEDS, MOTORSCOOTERS—see **BICYCLES**

N

NEWSPAPERS and MAGAZINES *(novine; časopis)*. Most leading western European newspapers, including British dailies and the American *International Herald Tribune* published in Paris, are sold at all major resorts. The papers usually arrive the day after publication. Popular foreign magazines are also sold at the same shops or stands.

Have you any English-language newspapers?	**Imate li novine na engleskom?**

P

PETS and VETS *(ljubimci-životinje; veterinar)*. Though *you* may not need a health certificate to enter Yugoslavia, your dog or cat won't be allowed across the border without one. This must attest to the animal's good health, include a vaccination record and affirm that you'll submit the pet to an examination by a Yugoslav vet at the border.

In many resort areas, if you need a vet you may find he's more attuned to the needs of mules and goats than chihuahuas.

Returning to Great Britain or Eire, your pet will have to undergo six months of quarantine. Both the USA and Canada reserve the right to impose quarantine.

PHOTOGRAPHY *(fotografisanje)*. You can buy film everywhere in Yugoslavia but to be sure of having your favourite brand, and to save on cost, bring your own supply from home. Photo shops in cities and even small towns advertise speedy developing. For colour film, though, it's probably faster to take your exposed film back home with you for development.

Certain areas—generally near military installations and national borders—are off limits to photographers. They're clearly marked with signs depicting an old-fashioned bellows camera crossed out with a diagonal red line.

The quaintly costumed people you may come across are usually quite accustomed to cameras. However, if you detect any embarrassment or annoyance, the decent course is to desist. One snapshot is scarcely worth an international incident. And less shy subjects are probably ready to be filmed around the next bend in the road.

Beware of lighting situations you might not have encountered before—especially the blinding reflections from the sea and white buildings. You may not be able to rely on the electric eye of your automatic camera in these situations. The secret is to compensate for the reflections with a faster shutter speed. Read your instruction book carefully or, before leaving home, talk over the problem with your camera dealer.

I'd like a film for this camera.	**Želim film za ovu kameru.**
a black-and-white film	**crno-beli film**
a colour film	**u boji [kolor] film**
a colour-slide film	**film za kolor dijapozitive**
35-mm film	**trideset pet milimetarski film**
super-8	**super osam**
How long will it take to develop (and print) this?	**Koliko vremena treba da se razvije film (i izrade fotografije)?**

P   **POLICE** *(milicija)*. The national police, armed and wearing grey-blue uniforms, maintain public order and control traffic. Each policeman's identity is revealed by his service number, clearly engraved on his belt buckle.

Where's the nearest police station?	**Gde je najbliža milicijska stanica?**

POST OFFICE and TELEGRAMS *(pošta; telegram)*. Post offices are identified by yellow *PTT* signs outside. Most post offices are open from 7 a.m. to 8 p.m. without a break though some have shorter hours. (Some post offices limit acceptance of registered mail to certain times; see posted hours.) Besides mail, post offices accept telegrams as well as long-distance telephone calls (see also TELEPHONE).

You can buy your stamps at tobacconists' and news-stands.

Airmail is recommended to all destinations unless time isn't essential. Registered letters and packages must be presented unsealed; the postal clerk will seal them in your presence.

Letter boxes in Yugoslavia, painted yellow, are usually affixed to house walls.

express (special delivery)	**ekspres**
airmail	**avionom**
registered	**preporučeno**
poste restante (general delivery)	**post restant**
A stamp for this letter/postcard, please.	**Molim Vas marku za ovo pismo/ za ovu kartu.**
I want to send a telegram to...	**Želim da pošaljem telegram za...**

PRICES. Inflation and prices in Yugoslavia have climbed vertiginously in the last years. But fortunately for the visitor, the dinar has been constantly devalued against Western currencies, and prices in Western terms have remained remarkably stable. It is best to take traveller's cheques in fairly low coupons, and only change as you need to. To give here any dinar prices would be misleading. The following figures in U.S. dollars give an approximate idea of the equivalent cost of items.

Camping. $3.50 per person per night, $1.50 for tent or car, $2 per caravan (trailer).

Car hire. *Renault 4* $12.50 per day, $0.13 per km., $168 per week with unlimited mileage. *Zastava 128* $16.50 per day, $0.17 per km., $231 per week with unlimited mileage. *VW Jetta* $24 per day, $0.24 per km., $308 per week with unlimited mileage. Add 15% tax and insurance.

Entertainment. Discotheque $1.70, cinema $0.85–1.70 depending on length of film, orchestral concerts $5–6, folklore performances $10 (transport included).

Hairdressers. *Woman's* shampoo and set $5, shampoo and blow-dry $6.75, permanent wave $8.50–13.50. *Man's* haircut $1.70–2.

Meals and drinks. Continental breakfast $3.50, 3-course set menu in hotel "A" category $11, coffee $0.70, Yugoslav brandy and spirits $1 (0.3 l.), litre of table wine $6.75, soft drinks $1.40–1.50.

Is there an admission charge?	**Koliko staje ulaz?**
Have you something cheaper?	**Imate li nešto jeftinije?**
How much?	**Koliko staje?**

PUBLIC HOLIDAYS *(državni praznik)*

Jan. 1, 2	*Nova godina*	New Year
May 1, 2	*Prvi maj*	Labour Days
July 4	*Dan borca*	Veterans' Day
Nov. 29, 30	*Dan Republike*	Republic Days

In addition, a Day of the Uprising *(Dan Ustanka)* is celebrated on July 22 in Slovenia and on July 27 in Croatia.

Are you open tomorrow?	**Da li je otvoreno sutra?**

RADIO and TV *(radio, televizija).* Two Yugoslav television channels serve the area. About half the programmes are in colour. Feature films are usually shown with the original sound-track and subtitles. You don't have to understand Serbo-Croatian to follow sports or musical shows.

On medium-wave radio, the local programmes of a good many European countries are easily picked up on any transistor. BBC and Voice of America programmes are heard most clearly on short wave in the early morning and at night. In summer, Zagreb radio has a daily English broadcast for tourists with news and helpful information.

S **SEAMSTRESSES** and **TAILORS** *(krojačica; krojač)*. If your clothing suddenly needs minor alterations, ask your hotel maid or desk-clerk to send it out for repairs. If you're more adventurous—or desperate—take the problem to the nearest town. There's no shortage of tailors; you can see them sewing in their ground-floor workrooms facing the street.

Could you mend this by tomorrow evening?	**Možete li popraviti ovo do sutra uveče?**

T **TAXIS** *(taksi)*. Clearly marked taxis are available at ranks in all towns and tourist centres, but tend to be rather expensive. Taxis in larger towns have meters, but in smaller places, where there may be only one taxi, ask about the fare in advance. Extra charges are levied for luggage and night travel. A 10 per cent tip would be appropriate.

What's the fare to...?	**Koliko košta do...?**

TELEGRAMS—see **POST OFFICES**

TELEPHONE *(telefon)*. Most towns have telephones on the street from which you may dial local calls by depositing 2 dinars.

For long-distance calls, the telephone office is located in the local post office. In most localities in Yugoslavia, you can dial direct to western Europe. Or, if you prefer, your hotel switchboard should be able to handle any calls, local or international.

If you're having difficulty spelling names, use this foolproof Yugoslavian telephone alphabet:

A	Avala	**F**	Foča	**N**	Niš	**V**	Valjevo
B	Beograd	**G**	Gorica	**Nj**	Njegoš	**Z**	Zagreb
C	Cetinje	**H**	Hercegovina	**O**	Osijek	**Ž**	Žirovnica
Č	Čačak	**I**	Istra	**P**	Pirot		
Ć	Ćuprija	**J**	Jadran	**R**	Rijeka		
D	Dubrovnik	**K**	Kosovo	**S**	Skopje	**Q**	Kvadrat
Dj	Djakovo	**L**	Lika	**Š**	Šibenik	**W**	Duplo V
Dž	Džamija	**Lj**	Ljubljana	**T**	Titograd	**X**	Iks
E	Evropa	**M**	Mostar	**U**	Uroševac	**Y**	Ipsilon